STUDENT UNIT G

UNIT

CCEA® A2 | 2

History

Partition of Ireland 1900–25 (Option 4)

Henry A. Jefferies

PHILIP ALLAN
UPDATES

Philip Allan Updates, an imprint of Hodder Education, an Hachette UK company, Market Place, Deddington, Oxfordshire OX15 0SE

Orders
Bookpoint Ltd, 130 Milton Park, Abingdon, Oxfordshire OX14 4SB
tel: 01235 827827
fax: 01235 400401
e-mail: education@bookpoint.co.uk
Lines are open 9.00 a.m.–5.00 p.m., Monday to Saturday, with a 24-hour message answering service. You can also order through the Philip Allan Updates website: www.philipallan.co.uk

© Henry A. Jefferies 2011

ISBN 978-1-4441-1259-7

First printed 2011
Impression number 5 4 3 2 1
Year 2015 2014 2013 2012 2011

This guide has been written specifically to support students preparing for the CCEA® A2 History Unit 2 examination, Option 4. The content has been fully approved and endorsed by CCEA.

CCEA is a registered trademark, the use of which has been licensed to Hodder Education.

Examination questions and specification information used with the permission of the Northern Ireland Council for the Curriculum, Examinations and Assessment. CCEA GCE Specification in History; CCEA Circular S-1F-49-10.

Typeset by MPS Limited, a Macmillan Company
Printed by MPG Books, Bodmin

Hachette UK's policy is to use papers that are natural, renewable and recyclable products and made from wood grown in sustainable forests. The logging and manufacturing processes are expected to conform to the environmental regulations of the country of origin.

Contents

Introduction

■ ■ ■

Content Guidance

■ ■ ■

Questions & Answers

Introduction

About this unit

Each option in History Unit A2 2 is worth 30% of CCEA's A-Level History course (60% of the A2 modules). It is assessed by means of a 120-minute examination during which you must:

- answer one compulsory question, in two parts, involving the evaluation and analysis of sources
- write one essay (from a choice of two) involving historical enquiry and interpretations

Historical investigations and interpretations

'Partition of Ireland 1900–25', like all the options in History Unit A2 2, requires you to adopt an investigative approach in your study. That means investigating specific questions, problems or issues raised by historians, and using historical sources to reach substantiated conclusions. More specifically, you should investigate why an event occurred or an issue arose, and examine its consequences. You must use contemporary evidence to support or underpin your answers. Historians' interpretations should also be used to inform the debate, and add depth and perspectives to your answers.

Assessing the partition of Ireland will involve you in evaluating sources you may not have seen before, so it is expected that you will have had the opportunity to evaluate a range of source materials as part of your study of this option. Each source must be explored and evaluated for its reliability and utility. You must examine each source with a view to interpreting its author's motive, its intended audience, what it indicates about causes and consequences, and its significance. You are expected to use the evidence of contemporary sources, historians' interpretations, and your own knowledge and judgement to arrive at well-argued conclusions about significant questions regarding the partition of Ireland. It is expected that you will have been given the opportunity to carry out independent research in this topic.

Assessment Objectives

In the examination of Unit A2 2, equal marks are awarded for the two Assessment Objectives (AO1 and AO2).

AO1 focuses on your ability to recall, select and deploy historical knowledge, and to communicate your knowledge and understanding in a clear and effective manner. You are expected to demonstrate your understanding of the past through careful analysis, coherent explanation and the presentation of convincing conclusions. You must show that you have mastered such key concepts in history as causation, consequence, change, continuity and significance. You should be able to discuss the connections between the key features of the period you have studied.

AO2 focuses on your ability to analyse and evaluate a range of source materials relevant to a historical enquiry. You must be able to comprehend, analyse and make judgements on different historians' interpretations of the topics you have studied.

Using historiography

The study of historians' interpretations is known as historiography. Historiography should be used in a meaningful way in answers to examination questions in this unit to enrich or illustrate a debate. It is not about name-dropping or including quotations in an answer which do not add to the debate.

You should practise using the names of contemporaries (groups/parties/ individuals) and historians whenever you are responding to questions assessing AO2. Contemporary evidence could be identified, for example, as a statement from an individual or party on the main issues you are discussing. It can be cited either as a direct quotation or by indirectly conveying its meaning. Historians' views or opinions could be included, for example, about key personalities or events in the period under discussion. You can also present this evidence directly or indirectly. Paraphrasing a historian's argument is acceptable. A balance in the number of references to contemporary and later interpretations is not required in a response.

Source evaluation and analysis

Question 1(a) reads:

Consult all the sources and your knowledge of this period. Which of the sources would an historian value most as evidence in a study of...?'

This question will assess AO2 — the skills of source evaluation and analysis. Contextual knowledge is expected in answers to this question. This question is worth 15 marks.

Question 1(b) reads:

Use all the sources and other evidence you have studied. How far do the sources support the view that...?'

Since this question assesses AO2 **and** AO1 it not only assesses your skills in source evaluation and analysis, but also your ability to use historical knowledge effectively in explaining, analysing and making judgements. This question is worth 20 marks — 10 marks are allocated to the assessment of AO2 and 10 marks are allocated to the assessment of AO1. Therefore, if you neglect to introduce 'other evidence' into your answer you cannot be awarded marks for this assessment objective, even if you have used all the sources in your response and provided an excellent evaluation and analysis.

The phrase 'How far...?' invites you to debate the extent to which the sources support a statement. You should use all the sources in your response. However, you must **also** use 'other evidence' to support your argument. This may take the form of factual, contemporary or historiographical knowledge. The use of historiography is **not** an absolute requirement or prerequisite for this question, but its use is likely to enhance your answers.

Historical interpretations

In this section of the examination paper, you are required to write a traditional essay worth 35 marks. Twenty of those marks are for Assessment Objective 1. That requires you to recall, select and deploy historical knowledge appropriately and to communicate it in a clear and effective manner. It also requires you to demonstrate an understanding of the past through explanation and analysis, and to form substantiated judgements. Fifteen of the marks awarded for the essay are allocated to Assessment Objective 2, the assessment of historical interpretations. Both contemporary **and** later interpretations are required. Contemporary material provides a rich source of evidence to discuss views, opinions and attitudes, while the views of historians are an ideal way for you to debate a topic. You will get marks for historical interpretation by including references to contemporary opinions regarding any of the issues being discussed and by including historiography or historians' interpretations. You will receive credit for offering interpretations of your own which attempt to assess the issues that are raised in the essay, but this will form part of the mark for 'knowledge' rather than 'interpretation'.

Mark scheme for the assessment of AO2 in Section B

Level	Characteristics of response
Level 1 (0–3)	Answers will reveal little or no awareness of contemporary or later interpretations of the subject.
Level 2 (4–7)	Answers at this level will have some awareness of contemporary or later interpretations of the subject, but this will be limited and in need of further development.
Level 3 (8–11)	Answers at this level will provide a satisfactory analysis and evaluation of either contemporary or later interpretations of the subject or a partial evaluation of both.
Level 4 (12–15)	Answers at this level will provide a good analysis and evaluation of contemporary and later interpretations of the subject.

Fifteen marks out of a total of 35 are allocated to the assessment of AO2.

In preparing to write a History essay you must first read the question carefully and ensure that you understand the proposition made by the question. In the light of your own knowledge and understanding of the subject of the question, you must think about the arguments for and against the proposition made by the question. You must decide which arguments are most compelling. Only then should you plan to write the essay, either agreeing or disagreeing with the proposition. In writing the essay, you are expected to acknowledge both sides of the debate, to show an awareness of different arguments and opinions. It may be that you only partially agree or disagree with the proposition made. Nonetheless, it is important that you present a clear and persuasive argument that mostly agrees with, or mostly disagrees with, the proposition.

In essay questions in which one factor is singled out as the most important one in explaining a development in history, you should address the nominated factor first and in detail before going on to deal with the other important factors. For example, in a question proposing, 'Religion was the most important factor in inspiring unionist opposition to Home Rule', you must first discuss the role of religion in unionism in depth, before considering the relative importance of other factors such as economic considerations, unionists' concerns about their British citizenship and identity, and the integrity of the UK and the British empire.

In writing any essay, you must be aware that top marks are awarded for the quality of the argument presented. You should indicate clearly in the introduction to the essay what its argument will be. The essay must remain focused on that argument throughout, and it is wise to 'echo the title' of the essay throughout. You must produce strong evidence to support or illustrate the argument being made. Marks are awarded not for the number of facts presented, but for the strength of the argument using those facts. Candidates often lose marks because they fail to provide enough evidence to support their argument convincingly, or because they present a lot of facts but fail to address the question posed. A good essay should address the question posed, presenting a clear argument which is supported by contemporary evidence and historians' interpretations.

When writing an essay with significant historiographical elements, you may punctuate it with references to the work of later historians and contemporary views of those who were involved or observers of events pertinent to the question, or you may decide to write a factual essay addressing the proposition followed by an assessment of contemporary and later interpretations. There is no preferred structure for answers to essay questions. You will be awarded marks which reflect the quality and coherence of your response in addressing the proposition.

How to use this guide

This guide is designed to help you with revision. It should be used in conjunction with other resources that you have used while studying this unit. You should be familiar with CCEA's online resources: specification, past examination papers and mark schemes. You are expected to have read at least some of the books on the resource list that follows. Reading will deepen your understanding of the subject and help you to appreciate the debates among historians about controversial aspects of this subject. You ought also to read any relevant articles in *History Ireland*, a magazine which is published every 2 months. In a unit that requires you to answer questions based on a number of sources, reading books and articles will help to improve your comprehension of the sources you will be examined on, and help to improve the quality of your writing. Ask your teacher for advice on what you should read. As a general rule you should concentrate on more up-to-date books or articles by leading historians.

Use this guide, and past examination papers, to give focus to your reading. Remember, the examination for this unit will not ask you for a simple narrative of events — it will demand that you present a convincing argument that is supported by facts **and** shows an awareness of different historians' views on the question. Before you begin to write an answer to any examination question you must be clear in your mind as to what your answer will be, what evidence you have to support it and what historiography is relevant to the question. When revising, use this guide to address the kinds of questions the examiners are likely to set for you.

Resource list

There is no prescriptive list of historians whose work must be used for this option, but CCEA has recommended the following books:

Bew, P. (1994) *Ideology and the Irish Question: Ulster Unionism and Irish Nationalism 1912–1916,* OUP.

Bew, P. (1996) *John Redmond,* Dundalgan Press.

Boyce, D. G. (1982) *Nationalism in Ireland,* Croom Helm.

Canning, P. (1985) *British Policy Towards Ireland 1921–1941,* OUP.

Caulfield, M. (1995) *The Easter Rebellion,* Gill & Macmillan.

Costello, F. (2002) *The Irish Revolution and its Aftermath 1916–1923,* Irish Academic Press.

Dwyer, T. R. (1998) *Big Fellow, Long Fellow: A Joint Biography of Collins and De Valera,* Gill & Macmillan.

Edwards, R. (1977) *Patrick Pearse: The Triumph of Failure,* Faber.

Foy, M. and Barton, B. (1999) *The Easter Rising,* Sutton.

Greaves, C. D. (1972) *The Life and Times of James Connolly,* Lawrence & Wishart.

Harkness, D. (1983) *Northern Ireland Since 1920*, Helicon.

Hopkinson, M. (1988) *Green Against Green: The Irish Civil War*, Gill & Macmillan.

Kee, R. (1972) *The Green Flag: A History of Irish Nationalism*, Weidenfeld.

Laffan, M. (1999) *The Resurrection of Ireland: The Sinn Féin Party 1916–1923*, CUP.

Lee, J. J. (1989) *Ireland 1912–1985: Politics and Society*, CUP.

Litton, H. (1995) *The Irish Civil War*, Wolfhound Press.

Lyons, F. S. L. (1973) *Ireland Since the Famine*, Fontana.

McDowell, R. B. (1970) *The Irish Convention 1917–18*, Routledge.

Mitchell, A. (1995) *Revolutionary Government in Ireland: Dáil Éireann 1919–1922*, Gill & Macmillan.

O'Leary, C. and Maume, P. (2004) *Controversial Issues in Anglo–Irish Relations 1910–1921*, Four Courts Press.

Pakenham, F. (1951) *Peace by Ordeal: An Account From First-hand Sources of the Negotiation and Signature of the Anglo–Irish Treaty of 1921*, Mercier Press.

Rees, R. (1998) *Ireland 1905–25*, Colourpoint.

Stewart, A. T. Q. (1981) *Edward Carson*, Gill & Macmillan.

Stewart, A. T. Q. (1967) *The Ulster Crisis: Resistance to Home Rule, 1912–14*, Faber.

Townshend, C. (2005) *Easter 1916: The Irish Rebellion*, Allen Lane.

Townshend, C. (1975) *The British Campaign in Ireland 1919–1921: The Development of Political and Military Policies*, OUP.

County map of Ireland

KEY

▮▮▮▮ Provincial boundary
∙∙∙∙∙∙ County boundary
▢ The six counties that became Northern Ireland

Content
Guidance

There are three divisions in the content requirements in this specification:

- Home Rule crisis, 1900–14: how it developed and how it was handled by the key parties involved in it.
- Political events, 1914–18: the impact of the First World War on Irish politics, the 1916 Rising, the decline of the Irish Parliamentary Party (IPP) and the rise of Sinn Féin and its republican aspirations.
- Events in Ireland, 1919–25: how efforts were made to resolve the 'Irish Question', the settlements of 1920 and 1921, and how successful they were.

The main emphasis in the course is how the differing viewpoints of the various parties to the Irish Question resulted in conflicting aspirations and political calculations that demanded compromises and accommodations.

Outline of topics

Home Rule crisis, 1900–14

Why did nationalists want Home Rule?

Why did unionists oppose Home Rule?

What was the attitude of the Liberals and Conservatives towards Home Rule?

How did the IPP secure the submission of the Third Home Rule Bill to Parliament?

How did the unionists and conservatives campaign against the Third Home Rule Bill?

How did Asquith's Liberal government handle the Home Rule crisis?

Winners and losers: Ulster and Southern Unionists; IPP; Liberals and Conservatives

Political events, 1914–18

What was the impact of the Great War on Irish politics?

What caused the 1916 Rising?

Why did Sinn Féin replace the IPP as the voice of Irish nationalists in the general election of December 1918?

Events in Ireland, 1919–25

How was the Anglo–Irish War of 1919–21 fought?

Government of Ireland Act (1920)

Why did the British government and Sinn Féin agree to a truce in July 1921?

Why did the Anglo–Irish Treaty of 1921 provoke a civil war?

What problems confronted the Northern Ireland government in the period 1920–25?

content guidance

Home Rule crisis, 1900–14
Why did nationalists want Home Rule?

D. George Boyce, in *Nationalism in Ireland*, accepts the general definition that nationalists are 'a group of people who consider themselves to be a nation'. In 1900 an Irish nationalist was one who identified with Ireland and the Irish nation, and with Irish forebears who had been conquered by English armies and subsequently had their lands confiscated and granted to English and Scottish Protestants (Irish Catholics owned only 4% of the land of Ireland by 1800), and endured centuries of anti-Catholic persecution under the British crown (the 'penal days'). Irish nationalists were never exclusively Catholic, but the terms 'Catholic' and 'nationalist' were almost synonymous in Ireland in 1900. Irish nationalists rejected the legitimacy of the Act of Union which created the United Kingdom of Great Britain and Ireland in 1801. They wanted the restoration of an Irish parliament with legislative powers to govern Ireland in the best interests of the Irish people. They supported the Irish Parliamentary Party (IPP), commonly known as the Irish Party or Home Rule Party, because it represented their aspirations in the UK Parliament. In 1886, 85 of Ireland's 105 MPs were elected to the Irish Party.

What was Home Rule?

Home Rule was the name given to a form of devolved government which would have established an Irish parliament and executive in Dublin with responsibility for strictly Irish affairs, while Ireland remained part of the UK and subject to the supreme authority of the British Parliament at Westminster. The originator of the concept of Home Rule, Isaac Butt MP, was an Ulster Protestant who recognised that the Act of Union between Great Britain and Ireland had not forged a 'union of hearts and minds'. He hoped to unite Irish people of different political outlooks and religions by empowering them to govern themselves in Ireland's best interests. Alvin Jackson observes in *Home Rule: An Irish History 1800–2000* that it was an ambiguous concept that bound together a wide spectrum of nationalist opinion: from those who, like John Redmond, leader of the IPP (1900–18), were content for Ireland to remain an integral part of the UK once it enjoyed a devolved government in Dublin, to the many separatists who wished to see Ireland completely free of British rule. Charles Stewart Parnell, the most outstanding leader of the IPP (1879–91), had declared in 1885, 'No man has the right to fix the boundary of the march of a nation.' Jackson, in *Home Rule*, characterises the concept of Home Rule as both ambiguous and appealing for nationalists, but its ambiguity fuelled unionists' fears about nationalists' long-term intentions.

Home Rule and religion

At first, Home Rule attracted considerable interest from Irish Protestant patriots such as Butt and Parnell. However, as politics became more democratic the IPP came increasingly to reflect the religious identity of the great majority of the Irish electorate, and consequently it became (predominantly but never exclusively) a party of Irish Catholics. Boyce points out that the Irish Party was not a 'sectarian party', but it very much reflected Irish Catholics' political and social concerns and aspirations.

The Land Question

The Land Question was a central issue of concern for the great majority of the men who voted for the IPP in the late nineteenth century. At the heart of this issue was the contested relationship between the landlords who owned the farmland of Ireland and the tenant farmers who rented their farms from them. Philip Bull has shown repeatedly, in *Land, Politics and Nationalism: A Study of the Irish Land Question* and elsewhere, that the 'Land Question' was intrinsically linked to the 'National Question' and that the IPP's engagement with the issue of land reform was an effective component of its wider nationalist strategy. It secured for the party a firm social base in Ireland's overwhelmingly rural constituencies. However, it made implacable enemies of the landlords, the richest and most powerful people in Ireland. Landlords held a great proportion of the most senior positions in the British government in Ireland, 75–80% according to C. S. Morley. Of the 751 members of the Grand Juries that governed Ireland's counties, 704 were Protestant unionists. Landlords demanded respect and deference on the basis of their landed wealth, as their peers enjoyed in Britain. However, Irish nationalists regarded them as an alien colonial clique whose land rightfully belonged to the Irish people.

Catholic aspirations

Most of the IPP's voters had farming backgrounds, but the party also represented the aspirations of other sections of Catholic society. The growing Catholic middle classes looked to Home Rule to remove what Alvin Jackson in *Home Rule* terms the 'glass ceiling' — 'the domination of the higher ranks of the professions and public service by the residual Irish Protestant elite or (worse still) by Englishmen'. Alan O'Day, in *Irish Home Rule, 1867–1921*, cites statistics showing that in 1900, although Catholics comprised 75% of the Irish population, only 43% of doctors, 44% of barristers and solicitors, and 59% of civil service officers were Catholics.

The Irish Party's continued demands in Westminster for equal employment opportunities in Ireland, and its successes in securing practical reforms in public service employment, won it support from the educated Catholic elites across Ireland. However, by threatening the privileged position of Protestants, the IPP reinforced their hostility towards Catholics. The Irish Party's support for the campaign for the establishment of a Catholic university in Ireland, to match the Protestant Trinity College, Dublin, reflected its commitment to representing Catholic aspirations at Westminster, but also had the effect of emphasising its denominational character.

New nationalism

The IPP was split between 1890 and 1900 after the Liberal Party insisted that Charles Stewart Parnell resign as leader of the Irish Party following scandalous revelations about his sexual relations with the wife of a fellow MP. Liberal support was essential if Home Rule was to be secured, but nationalists were split as to whether Parnell, 'the uncrowned king of Ireland', should resign to placate British moralists.

According to W. B. Yeats, whose view was echoed by Irish historians such as F. S. L. Lyons until recent times, the split in the Irish Party fed a disillusionment with nationalist politics that opened the way for a 'New Nationalism'. However, Yeats' biographer Roy Foster has shown that Yeats was very much influenced by a cultural flowering that was already underway and reflected in the Young Ireland societies and the *Dublin University Review*, not to mention the extremely popular Gaelic Athletic Association (GAA) (founded in 1884). Foster and other leading historians, including Boyce and Jackson, do not see the cultural revival as a challenge to parliamentary politics, but as complementary to it. Patrick Maume has shown that many members of the Irish Party were supportive of the cultural movement and became advocates on its behalf.

The Gaelic League, established in 1893 by Douglas Hyde and Eóin Mac Néill, succeeded in raising nationalists' appreciation of the Irish language and culture generally, but it failed to revive the language beyond the classroom. Yeats and a small group of other writers and dramatists sought to create an Irish national literature and drama in the English language that would further the national cause while exercising an international artistic appeal and credibility. They succeeded in producing work of international renown and regard. However, Boyce has drawn attention to the far greater strength of the popular nationalist literature of the time, which eschewed the Gaelic League's dream of fostering a Gaelic Ireland, as well as the visions of a mythical Celtic past promoted by Yeats and his elitist Anglo–Irish clique. Popular nationalism was stubborn and sentimental, Catholic and conservative, with a deep affection for Ireland and Irish people's localities. Senia Pesata has shown that even among the best-educated young Catholics, 'Gaelicist politics' were marginal before 1916.

Strengths and weaknesses of the IPP

Historians have debated the relative strengths and weaknesses of the IPP. There is agreement that the Parnellite split contributed to a 'slow-burning disillusionment' with parliamentary politics in some circles. Nonetheless, the Irish Party was reunited in 1900 against the background of a surge in nationalist sentiment against Britain's Boer War in South Africa. The new leader, John Redmond, is characterised by Jackson as 'an able, kindly but highly defensive commander...chosen in 1900 as much because of his political weaknesses as because of his strengths'. Yet his weaknesses were less apparent than his strengths in the early years of the twentieth century.

Recent studies by Pesata and Maume, endorsed by Boyce and Jackson, have found that the Irish Party was successful and vibrant at the start of the twentieth century. It had 'sole rights' to the popular cause of Home Rule and faced no credible challenges from within the nationalist community. It survived the decades of failure to secure Home Rule by promoting nationalist causes and reflecting Catholic aspirations effectively at Westminster. By 1900 it was also benefiting from a growing conviction among Catholics in Ireland, and an acceptance (however grudging) among an increasing number of people in Great Britain, that some form of Home Rule was inevitable. A fatal weakness, though, was its failure to address unionist opposition effectively. There were many nationalists, including John Dillon, deputy leader of the Irish Party, who feared that any compromise with unionists could undermine the campaign for Home Rule.

Why did unionists oppose Home Rule?

Unionists supported the Act of Union that had bound Ireland to Great Britain in the United Kingdom since 1801. They opposed Home Rule for fear of the consequences of being subject to a government of Irish Catholics. They were fearful about what would become of their 'civil and religious liberties', their economic wellbeing, their British citizenship and identity and their place in the British empire if, as they suspected, Irish nationalists were to use Home Rule as a stepping stone to independence from the UK at some point in the future.

Irish unionism

At first the unionist opposition to Home Rule encompassed the whole of Ireland. Since only the richest 4.4% of the people in Ireland were allowed to vote in parliamentary elections until 1885, wealthy Protestant landlords, large farmers, businessmen and professionals were able to elect a very disproportionate number of Ireland's MPs. The landlords, predominantly members of the Protestant Church of Ireland, considered themselves to be Ireland's natural ruling class by right of their tremendous landed wealth and titles. They dominated the senior positions in the British government in Ireland, and were prominent in Irish business too. Overwhelmingly they were supporters of the Conservative Party and had close social and political ties with English landed families. Around 144 members of the House of Lords at Westminster in the Home Rule era were landlords in Ireland. Irish landlords, such as Lord Lansdowne, used some of their wealth, power and influence to oppose Home Rule, in the UK Parliament and beyond.

The results of the 1886 general election were a shock for Irish unionists. With the right to vote extended to 16% of the population, the election was much more democratic than ever before. Only 17 Conservative MPs were elected, as against 85 Home Rule MPs. These results showed that unionists could only win elections in constituencies where most of the people were Protestants. Protestants formed

54% of the population of Ulster, but only 9% of the population of the three southern provinces.

Southern unionists formed the Irish Loyal and Patriotic Union in 1885 to oppose Home Rule. Ulster unionists formed the Ulster Loyalist Union in 1886. Both organisations were dominated by landlords. Despite the fact that the southern unionists could not hope to win elections (except for Dublin South), they were influential within the Conservative Party, especially in the House of Lords. Southern Irish Unionists sometimes campaigned in Britain against Home Rule. Most of the unionist MPs from Ulster were also landlords. Landlords dominated the Ulster Loyalist Union and took leadership positions in the Orange Order in order to mobilise poorer Protestants against Home Rule.

Unionist landlords

For the landlords, the struggle against Home Rule was a struggle to defend their 'natural' position as the ruling class of Ireland. They were frightened by the nationalist challenge to their ownership of the land of Ireland and the IPP's increasing identification with the aspirations of Catholic tenant farmers. In other words, the landlords were driven by a concern to protect their own wealth, power and privileges. They were fearful about the possible consequences of Home Rule for the civil and religious rights of Protestants under a predominantly Catholic government. As members of the Conservative elites, Irish landlords were fearful too about the future of the UK, and indeed of the entire British empire, if Irish nationalists were to progress towards an independent Ireland. The Irish Unionist Parliamentary Party was founded in 1886 by Edward Saunderson, a landlord from County Cavan. It was dominated by landlords committed to all-Ireland unionism.

The Orange Order

In order to mobilise Protestant voters behind the unionist cause the unionist landlords looked to the Orange Order. This body united Protestants of different denominations, chiefly Church of Ireland and Presbyterians, in opposition to Irish Catholics. The Order was more sectarian than most of the unionist leaders in Westminster, but the utility of the Order for mobilising Protestant voters far outweighed its liabilities. Alvin Jackson, in *Ireland: 1798–1998*, observes that 'the significance of the Orange Order in terms of the ideological and institutional groundwork for Unionism can hardly be overstated'.

Orange hostility to Catholics had a number of roots. First and foremost was an instinctive hatred of the Pope and the Catholic religion. It was a detestation grounded in theological disputes, and also in folk memories of religious conflicts in history that were kept alive by the Orange Order, the Apprentice Boys clubs and similar organisations. The violent reaction of unionist mobs in Belfast to the introduction of the First Home Rule Bill to Parliament in 1886, in which 36 people were killed, was summed up in the slogan, 'Home Rule is Rome Rule.'

In addition, the scale of British immigration into Ulster was so much greater than it had been in the rest of Ireland that the process of dispossession and degradation of Catholics was more thorough in the north of Ireland than elsewhere. Whereas the great majority of the farmland in the south was rented by Catholic tenant farmers, most farmland in Ulster was rented by tenants who were Presbyterians or members of the Church of Ireland. Catholics tended to be confined to small farms on poor-quality land, or to be landless labourers. Catholics who migrated to Belfast and other northern towns faced religious discrimination, even from public bodies such as the Belfast Corporation, which kept them confined to the lowest-paid jobs, or no job at all. Poverty and its consequences, which included limited access to education, created another barrier between Catholics and their Protestant neighbours. It also encouraged many Protestants to feel superior to Catholics. The IPP's campaigns against religious discrimination in employment, and its association with the Ancient Order of Hibernians, a Catholic organisation that sought to redress the discrimination suffered by Catholics, reinforced Protestants' fears about the consequences of Home Rule.

Economic considerations

Belfast's Protestant businessmen, and their mainly Protestant employees, saw Home Rule as posing a direct threat to their economic wellbeing. It was widely assumed that an Irish government might introduce protectionist measures to support small Irish companies from competition from their larger British counterparts. Northern businessmen and their employees worried that protectionist measures introduced by a Home Rule government could result in British counter-measures that would undermine Belfast's export-orientated industries, including its shipbuilding, engineering and textile firms. In addition, Ulster businessmen were fearful that their companies might be taxed in order to subsidise poor districts in the west of Ireland.

British identity

Paul Bew, in *Ideology and the Irish Question*, acknowledges the central role of religion in the unionist campaign against Home Rule, but he also highlights non-sectarian motives underlying unionism. These were not confined to economic considerations. He emphasises the importance of unionists' British identity as a fundamental reason for their opposition to Home Rule, and highlights the fact that many Ulster unionist leaders had been educated in England and shared the wider outlook of Britain's elites.

The unionist case against Home Rule was concisely summarised in the Solemn League and Covenant of 1912. Its very title was chosen to remind people of the covenant between God and his 'chosen people' in the Bible, and of the struggles of Scottish Protestants during the Reformation. The language of the 1912 covenant was Protestant in tone, and explicitly called on God to protect Protestants then as he had succoured their ancestors in 'days of stress and trial'. The 1912 covenant made the place of religion in unionism very clear. It highlighted unionists' fears for their 'civil and religious liberties' under an Irish government, their anxieties for the economic wellbeing of Ireland, and the threat they perceived to their 'cherished position of equal citizenship in the United Kingdom'. Protestantism was central to unionists' sense of identity, as British subjects loyal to the Crown, in opposition to Irish Catholic nationalists.

How did British political parties address the issue of Home Rule?

Liberal alliance

In 1886 W. E. Gladstone, the leader of the Liberal Party, announced his commitment to the cause of Home Rule for Ireland. After forming an alliance with the IPP, Gladstone submitted the First Home Rule Bill to Parliament in 1886, only to see it defeated in the House of Commons. Gladstone's Second Home Rule Bill was passed by the Commons in 1893, but it was resoundingly defeated by 419 votes to 41 in the Conservative- and unionist-dominated House of Lords. From 1895 to 1906 the Conservatives and unionists formed the government of the UK, and the issue of Home Rule took a back seat at Westminster. After Gladstone's retirement, no Liberal leader was as committed to Home Rule as he had been.

Conservative and unionist opposition to Home Rule

Alvin Jackson has emphasised the possibility that the Conservative Party might have been prepared to consider Home Rule for Ireland in 1885/86. Even Lord Randolph Churchill, who coined the phrase 'Ulster will fight and Ulster will be right', gave positive thought to the possibility of Home Rule. However, once Gladstone had committed the Liberal Party to Home Rule, the Conservatives set themselves against it. Yet, there was more to the Conservatives' commitment to unionism than party politics. Irish unionists comprised a significant minority of the Conservative and unionist bloc in Parliament: one-eighth of MPs in 1906 and a much larger fraction in the Lords. The Conservatives were the party most committed to British imperialism, and Irish nationalism was seen as a threat to the integrity of both the UK and the British empire.

From 1893 to 1906 the Conservative and unionist government tried to prove that there was no need for Home Rule by providing good government from Westminster, a policy called 'killing Home Rule with kindness'. A series of Land Acts was passed, the most important being the Wyndham Land Act (1903), which effectively resolved the Land Question by facilitating tenant farmers in purchasing their farms from the landlords with repayable government loans. The poverty besetting the western counties of Ireland was tackled through the establishment of the Congested Districts Board in 1890. A Department of Agriculture was established in Dublin to oversee that key area of the Irish economy. The Local Government Reform Act of

1898 established virtually democratic urban and county councils in Ireland in place of the landlord-dominated Grand Juries. In the 1899 elections, 551 nationalists were elected to councils across Ireland, as against 124 unionists (86 of those in Ulster). Some limited measures were introduced to curb religious discrimination in the public service.

Historians have debated the merits of the policy of 'kindness'. Boyce reckons that it was not pursued with the energy or money needed to succeed, though Alan O'Day points out that it had a greater effect for good in Ireland than any previous government policies. The key fact, as Boyce emphasises in *Nationalism in Ireland*, is that nationalism was not just about grievances but also about a strong sense of Irish identity that demanded institutional form. The desire for Home Rule was not killed by kindness.

Ulster Unionist Council

Irish unionists were increasingly alienated by the Conservatives' 'kindness' policy because it seemed to favour nationalists. They reacted with outrage to the proposal for an Irish Council, a limited devolution scheme devised in 1904. A new generation of Ulster unionists, who were unhappy at the complacent leadership provided by Edward Saunderson and his landlord clique, took advantage of the devolution controversy to seize control of Ulster unionism. In March 1905 they set up the Ulster Unionist Council to reorganise and revitalise unionism in Ulster. The Council comprised 200 members, including 50 MPs and peers, 100 representatives of Unionist Associations in Ulster's constituencies, and 50 representatives of the Orange Order. Though landlords still comprised a third of the standing committee of the Ulster Unionist Council in 1910, it was dominated by representatives of Belfast's business and professional classes, and Orangemen.

The formation of the Ulster Unionist Council helped to lay the groundwork for the mass mobilisation of Ulster unionism during the Third Home Rule Bill crisis in the period 1910–14. Its role in splitting Irish unionism in two is debated, but Alvin Jackson's assessment is that the establishment of the Ulster Unionist Council was 'a hesitant but still vital step towards the creation of a distinctive northern movement'. It reflected a more provincial unionism, one that was self-confident and not entirely trustful of its Conservative allies, who seemed so ready to pander to the nationalists. It also reflected a realisation that the Conservative and unionist government faced certain defeat in the next general election.

Liberal government

The new Liberal government under Prime Minister Campbell-Bannerman, formed after the Liberals' landslide victory in the 1906 general election, favoured a step-by-step approach to the Irish Question, not unlike that of the previous Conservative government. Indeed, D. G. Boyce, in *The Irish Question and British Politics, 1868–1986*, claims that Britain's main political parties were moving towards an 'unofficial bipartisanship' on Ireland in the early years of the twentieth century. The Liberals'

Irish Council Bill of 1907 was closely modelled on the limited devolution scheme put together under the Conservative chief secretary for Ireland, Wyndham, in 1904.

However, Boyce reckons that when the nationalists rejected the Liberals' Council Bill as inadequate, following the unionists' earlier rejection of an almost identical Conservative proposal as too radical, it ended the prospect of any bipartisan approach in Westminster to Ireland. He argues too that the reformist policies of both the Conservatives and the Liberals had effectively addressed nationalists' grievances on the Land Question, local government and education, and there was little scope left for further concessions to appease the nationalists. By 1910 only the central nationalist demand for Home Rule remained to be resolved, while unionists in Ireland opposed the granting of any form of devolved government.

John Redmond, leader of the IPP, was able to exploit developments at Westminster to secure the enactment of the Third Home Rule Bill in September 1914. However, the passions enflamed by a wider constitutional crisis across the UK strengthened the hand of the Ulster unionists and ensured that they were able to block the establishment of a Home Rule government in Dublin.

How did the IPP secure the submission of the Third Home Rule Bill to Parliament?

The Parliament Act of 1911

Herbert Asquith, Liberal prime minister from April 1908, and David Lloyd George, chancellor of the exchequer, were determined to implement radical social reforms that would benefit poorer people in Britain. These reforms had to be paid for from increased taxation. In the 'People's Budget' of 1909 the Liberal government planned to increase income taxes for the rich, and introduce a land tax and an inheritance tax — two taxes that would hit landlords extremely hard. Inevitably, the Conservative and Unionist Party, which represented the interests of the landlords and other rich people, was furious. Its leaders saw the 'People's Budget' as an attack on Britain's natural ruling class (themselves) and consequently as a threat to the British system of government. They used their control of the House of Lords to veto the budget. That forced the Liberal government to call a general election in January 1910 in order to secure a mandate from the voters to have the budget enacted.

John Redmond promised the IPP's support for the Liberals, but only in return for an assurance that Ireland would finally be granted Home Rule. Asquith agreed. In the general election of January 1910 the number of Liberal MPs elected fell to 275, just ahead of the Conservatives with 273 MPs. Prime Minister Asquith also enjoyed the support of 40 Labour Party MPs. However, he needed the support of the Irish Party to remain in power. After the election Redmond made it clear to Asquith that the Irish Party would only support him on condition that the Lords' veto be abolished, and Home Rule be granted to Ireland. While most historians, including Patrick O'Farrell and Roy Foster, consider that Redmond was unable to influence the Liberals, Cornelius O'Leary and Patrick Maume, in *Controversial Issues*, point to his role in having the Lords' veto abolished as proof that he was not as powerless as others assumed.

Asquith persuaded King George V to promise to create enough Liberal lords in the House of Lords to outvote the Conservatives and unionists there, but the king told Asquith to call a second general election to secure a popular mandate for such an important constitutional reform. The Liberal, Labour and Irish parties campaigned to win the public's support to abolish the Lords' veto, pass the 'People's Budget' and give Home Rule to Ireland. The Conservatives and unionists realised that most voters supported the 'People's Budget', so they fought the election campaign mainly on the issue of Home Rule. They argued that Home Rule would inevitably lead to Irish independence and the break-up of the UK and the entire British empire. In the event, the Conservatives and unionists actually lost an MP in the general election held in December 1910. Nicholas Mansergh, in *The Unresolved Question: The Anglo–Irish Settlement and its Undoing, 1912–72*, remarks, 'By the end of 1910 Redmond had almost every cause for satisfaction.' In August 1911 Asquith's government passed the Parliament Act. It abolished the Lords' veto, though it allowed the Lords to delay the enactment of bills by up to 2 years. This opened the way for Home Rule.

The Third Home Rule Bill, 1912–14

The Government of Ireland Bill, as the Third Home Rule Bill was called officially, was given its first reading in the House of Commons on 11 April 1912. Its first clause emphasised that the 'supremacy' of the British Parliament would be 'unaffected and undiminished' by Home Rule. It defined those strictly Irish affairs that would come under the jurisdiction of a devolved Irish government, which (crucially) did not include taxation, and it indicated that the Irish government would be funded by means of an annual block grant from the British exchequer. All Irish legislation would be subject to the veto of the British Parliament and Crown. As Alvin Jackson observes, 'It was a painfully modest grant of legislative autonomy.' Nonetheless, for nationalists it promised to give institutional form to their deep-rooted sense of nationality. O'Leary and Maume have found that even in their private correspondence, Irish Party MPs regarded Home Rule as 'in the bag' and 'ignored the dangerous potentialities of Ulster Unionism'.

How did Redmond address the Ulster unionists' challenge?

F. S. L. Lyons criticises Redmond for being 'naïve in the extreme' in his management of the crisis that unfolded. Joe Lee, in *Ireland 1912–1985,* concurs, seeing Redmond as 'too much a romantic Commonwealth man, too much a genuine Westminster parliamentarian, to conceive that the Ulster Unionists, much less the English Tories... could really contemplate rebellion'. Robert Kee, in *The Bold Fenian Men*, criticises

Redmond for allowing himself to be completely dependent on the Liberals without recognising the dangers of such dependency. He simply trusted Asquith to deliver Home Rule.

Mansergh, in *The Unresolved Question*, reveals that Redmond and the other Irish Party MPs were isolated from the members of the Liberal government. They communicated through Augustine Birrell, the chief secretary for Ireland, but they had no personal relationship with Asquith, nor with any other key figure in the government. That was, as Jackson, in *Ireland*, and Mansergh point out, an enormous handicap once Lloyd George and Churchill took increasing control of the government's Irish policy. Redmond's isolation meant that he did not realise there were important divisions in the government about its Irish policy. He failed to see that the Liberal government was under pressure from the weight of public opinion in Britain. When, in February 1914, Asquith informed him that major concessions were needed to address the Ulster question, Redmond was so taken by surprise that, in Asquith's words, he 'shivered visibly and was a good deal perturbed'.

Bew, in his biography of John Redmond, shows that the Irish leader did not ignore the unionists' opposition. He repeatedly tried to reassure them in speeches and in newspaper articles that their fears were unfounded. Yet Redmond had no idea of the strength of Ulster unionist feeling. Possibly his personal experiences with southern unionists, whose small numbers inclined them to be more willing to compromise and less sectarian than their northern fellows, might have given him a misleading impression about the possibilities for reasoned debate and cooperation. His own mother was a Protestant and a unionist. In addition, Redmond was influenced by his two key lieutenants, John Dillon, deputy leader of the Irish Party, and Joe Devlin, the leading northern nationalist. Both of those men encouraged Redmond to dismiss the Ulster unionists' threats as bluff.

Éamon Phoenix, in *Northern Nationalism: Nationalist Politics, Partition and the Catholic Minority in Northern Ireland, 1890–1940*, shows that Devlin misled Redmond as to the gravity of the situation, perhaps because he underestimated the Ulster unionists himself, but also because he feared the consequences of partition for the people he represented, the Catholic minority in the northeast of Ireland. For Catholics in Ulster, Home Rule was seen as offering their only hope for equal rights and justice in the future.

Nonetheless, there is a feeling that Redmond ought to have recognised the scale of the Ulster unionist challenge and taken steps to address it. The All-for-Ireland League argued for greater efforts to be made to conciliate Irish Protestants. Maume has pointed out that Tim Healy, a dissident nationalist MP, recognised the strength of Ulster unionist hostility and foresaw the likelihood of partition. Diarmaid Ferriter, in *The Transformation of Ireland*, points to another nationalist, named Cleary, who also recognised the likelihood of partition and wondered whether excluding the Ulster Protestants from Home Rule would be a good thing. There is, of course, the probability that there was nothing Redmond could have said or done to assuage Ulster unionist hostility to Home Rule. With hindsight, it could be that the best that

Redmond might have worked towards was to minimise the number of Ulster counties to be excluded from Home Rule. However, he was genuinely appalled at the idea of partition and, like Asquith, he thought it was best to leave any concessions to the unionists for the last minute.

How did the Ulster unionists campaign against the Third Home Rule Bill?

Walter Long, the leader of the Irish unionist MPs, lost his seat in the January 1910 general election. In his place the Irish unionists elected Sir Edward Carson MP as their leader. Carson, a Protestant from Dublin, was one of the two MPs for Trinity College, Dublin. At the time he was England's solicitor-general, and an outstanding lawyer. He still had some family and friends in Dublin, and his intention was to stop any part of Ireland getting Home Rule. He decided to campaign on the usual unionist fears that Home Rule would destroy the UK and threaten the very survival of the British empire, issues that were bound to get sympathy from Conservative and unionist politicians and supporters in Great Britain. However, he recognised that a great many British voters had grown indifferent to the debate on Home Rule. Therefore he added a new dimension to the debate by highlighting its weakest point: the opposition of a majority of people in Ulster. All historians who have studied Carson, including A. T. Q. Stewart, Alvin Jackson and Russell Rees, agree that he took up the leadership of the Ulster unionists to prevent any part of Ireland securing Home Rule. It was only subsequently that he argued in favour of partition.

Sir James Craig, MP for East Down, invited Carson to visit Ulster and open the anti-Home Rule campaign. Carson had only ever been to Ulster once before. He responded to Craig by observing that he needed to be reassured 'that the people there really mean to resist. I am not for a mere game of bluff and, unless men are prepared to make great sacrifices which they clearly understand, the talk of resistance is no use....' Craig, a consummate organiser, staged a demonstration of commitment by 50,000 Orangemen and other unionists in the grounds of his house at Craigavon on 23 September 1911 to impress Carson. Carson responded with passionate oratory in which he demanded, 'We must be prepared..., the morning Home Rule passes, ourselves to become responsible for the government of the Protestant province of Ulster.' Alvin Jackson sees the Ulster Unionist Council as providing the foundations for an Ulster unionist provisional government: it was self-reliant, militant and willing to adopt extra-parliamentary means. By the early summer of 1911, Ulster unionist extremists had already smuggled 2,000 weapons into Ireland.

The campaign for 'Protestant Ulster'

Focusing on 'Protestant Ulster' was a very astute move by Carson. It aroused British public opinion to support the Protestant unionists against the Catholic nationalists at a time when, as Daniel Jackson points out in *Popular Opposition to Irish Home Rule in Edwardian Britain*, there was still a great deal of latent anti-Catholic and anti-Irish sentiment in Great Britain. If successful, it would confront the IPP with the choice of either abandoning the campaign for Home Rule or seeing Ireland partitioned. However, Carson was not yet committed to a partition settlement. He told a meeting of southern unionists in Dublin on 10 October 1911, 'If Ulster succeeds, Home Rule is dead.' In private correspondence in November 1911 he explained his rationale: any proposal by the Liberal government to partition Ireland would be rejected by the nationalists, and he expected them to simply accept the status quo. Patrick Maume, in *The Long Gestation: Irish Nationalist Life, 1891–1918*, has shown, however, that nationalists felt too strongly by that time to abandon their aspirations to self-government, especially when those aspirations seemed so very close to realisation.

Andrew Bonar Law

Carson's leadership of Irish unionism was a major boost for the Ulster unionists. So too was the appointment of Andrew Bonar Law as the new leader of the Conservative and Unionist Party in place of Arthur Balfour in November 1911. Bonar Law was born in Canada to a father who had been a Presbyterian minister in Coleraine, County Londonderry. Robert Blake, in his biography *The Unknown Prime Minister: The Life and Times of Andrew Bonar Law, 1858–1923*, shows that Bonar Law had a passionate attachment to Ulster and was more than happy to endorse Carson's Ulster strategy in the fight against Home Rule. Mansergh, in *The Unresolved Question*, agrees and argues that Bonar Law's becoming Conservative leader was crucial in the Third Home Rule Bill crisis. No other Conservative would have 'entered into an open-ended commitment to Carson and the Ulster unionists, let alone assail the government in such strident tones'. However, it also suited Bonar Law and the Conservative and Unionist Party leadership to focus their attentions entirely on the fight against Home Rule and away from their deep divisions about other policy issues, such as tariff reform.

Bonar Law's personal attachment was strictly to Ulster, but among the Conservative and unionist leadership there were important advocates for the southern unionists too, most notably Lord Lansdowne, the Conservative and Unionist leader in the House of Lords, and Walter Long, who was a leading figure in the Commons. Bonar Law made his first important speech on Home Rule in the Albert Hall, London, on 26 January 1912. He claimed that the Liberals were guilty of holding on to power through a corrupt bargain with the nationalists. Michael Laffan, in *The Partition of Ireland 1911–1925*, observes that the repeated Conservative and unionist claims that it was illegitimate for a Liberal government to look for nationalist support reflected their perspective wherein Irish nationalists were regarded as lesser citizens than unionists. Joe Lee, in *Ireland 1912–1985*, goes further and argues that Ulster unionists had a *Herrenvolk* mentality, a sense of racial superiority, that made them reject the idea that 'one Protestant be equated with one Catholic'.

On 9 April 1912 Bonar Law and Carson, flanked by several British as well as Ulster unionist MPs, addressed a crowd of 100,000 at the Balmoral showgrounds in Belfast. Bonar Law declared that the unionists were fighting to save the British empire. The implicit threat of violence was clear. Two days later Prime Minister Asquith submitted the Third Home Rule Bill to the House of Commons. It offered no concessions to placate the Ulster unionists' hostility, though Asquith was at great pains to emphasise that the bill did not in any way diminish the 'supreme authority' of the British Parliament. The Conservative and Unionist Party castigated the government's legislation as the product of a 'corrupt bargain' between the Liberals and the Irish nationalists.

The Ulster unionists fought a determined campaign to win British public opinion to their side. Alan O'Day, in *Irish Home Rule*, highlights the fact that they distributed 6 million booklets in Great Britain, organised almost 9,000 public meetings and canvassed nearly 1.5 million voters in marginal constituencies. Daniel Jackson, in *Popular Opposition to Irish Home Rule*, has shown that Carson, in particular, was accorded tremendous respect in many parts of Britain where Protestant and imperial sentiments were strongest. In March 1913 Baron Willoughby de Broke, a fierce opponent of the Parliament Act, launched the British League for the Support of Ulster and the Union and won wide support from British establishment figures and lesser mortals. It was becoming increasingly clear that the fate of Protestant Ulster was dominating the debate about Home Rule.

Prime Minister Asquith visited Dublin on 20 July 1912 to demonstrate his commitment to Home Rule. Bonar Law responded the following weekend with an inflammatory speech at Blenheim Palace in England in which he stated that Ulster Protestants would be justified in resisting Home Rule 'by all means in their power, including force', and he declared that he could imagine 'no length of resistance to which Ulster can go in which I would not be prepared to support them'. Bonar Law and Carson deliberately ratcheted up the violent feelings of the opponents of Home Rule. They undoubtedly provoked sectarian violence in Belfast, though Bew argues that the sectarian violence threatened to dent Carson's credibility in Britain. Blake and Mansergh point out that Bonar Law's violent rhetoric reflected his own peculiar attachment to Ulster, and did not reflect the general feeling in the Conservative and Unionist Party of which he was the leader. While the 'fighting talk' was popular among some backbenchers, it was not well received by all leading Conservatives.

Solemn League and Covenant

The Solemn League and Covenant was designed by Craig to inject further momentum into the Ulster unionist cause. The covenant was a binding agreement with God, modelled on the Old Testament covenant between God and his 'chosen people', and echoed the 1580 Scottish covenant in support of the Reformation. It outlined the economic and civil rights concerns of its signatories in relation to Home Rule, but put the spotlight on their religious concerns. It professed loyalty to 'his gracious majesty King George V', but warned that they would 'use all means that may be found necessary to defeat the present conspiracy to set up a Home Rule parliament in Ireland'. It called on God to help his people in their latest time of trial. Protestant church leaders were prominent in leading the signing of the covenant and, reflecting the religious emphasis of Ulster unionism, six of the first nine signatories were Protestant clergymen. The covenant itself incorporated the mix of motives inspiring Ulster unionists' opposition to Home Rule but, as Bew points out, it reflected the importance of the religious motive. In all, 218,000 men signed the covenant in Ulster, and 228,000 women signed a corresponding declaration. It was a tremendous propaganda success, making clear the strength of Ulster unionist determination to resist the imposition of Home Rule upon them.

Newspapers illustrated with photographs reported the proceedings on 'Ulster Day' across the UK. Indeed, on the morning after Ulster Day Carson was greeted by a crowd of no fewer than 150,000 people at Liverpool, another sectarian cauldron. The business leaders among the Ulster unionists used their experience in marketing to very good effect — creating the illusion of an Ulster that was resolutely opposed to Home Rule, despite the fact that almost half of the people of Ulster and its MPs were nationalists. Churchill scoffed at Carson publicly as the king of half-Ulster — but in the public mind in Britain the illusion of a uniformly Protestant Ulster was firmly established.

The exclusion of Ulster from Home Rule

To maintain the momentum gained, on 1 January 1913 Carson proposed an amendment to the Home Rule Bill to exclude the province of Ulster. It was, he reassured southern unionists, a tactical amendment and he had no wish to partition Ireland. However, thanks to his campaign, Conservative and unionist sentiment in Great Britain came to focus almost exclusively on the Ulster unionists' hostility to the prospect of being subject to an Irish and Catholic government. Carson may not have realised it, but his approach to the Third Home Rule Bill crisis made partition increasingly probable.

Ulster Volunteer Force

In January 1913 Carson endorsed the establishment of the Ulster Volunteer Force (UVF), though Jackson suggests that he was ambiguous about the use of violence to achieve political ends. The UVF was organised as a military force under a full-time headquarters staff of former British Army officers led by Lieutenant General Sir George Richardson. It drilled with dummy rifles at first, though thousands of Orangemen had already acquired guns illegally. The threat of violence was clear — but it was not clear who, in fact, the UVF would fight.

Any confrontation between the unionist paramilitaries and the British Army, or the Royal Irish Constabulary, would not only be 'suicidal' literally, but it would also undermine the support enjoyed by the Ulster unionists among many of the British public. On the other hand, should members of the UVF indulge in sectarian attacks on their Catholic neighbours, they also ran the risk of alienating British opinion. Nonetheless, the UVF was very significant as a reflection of Ulster unionist determination to resist Home Rule. Michael Laffan has pointed out that it was very significant too in 'putting the gun back into Irish politics'. The IPP had convinced Irish nationalists over several decades to trust constitutional politics to realise their aspirations. However, the Ulster unionists' use of the threat of armed force persuaded a growing number of advanced nationalists that British governments only heeded threats of violence, and were inclined to ignore nationalist arguments that were promoted peacefully. Unwittingly, Carson strengthened a republican tradition that had been eclipsed by the campaign for Home Rule since the 1870s.

How did Asquith's Liberal government handle the Home Rule crisis?

Historians are divided in their assessment of Prime Minister Asquith's handling of the Third Home Rule Bill crisis. Patricia Jalland, in *The Liberals and Ireland: The Ulster Question in British Politics to 1914*, criticises Asquith for his 'wait and see' policy. She argues that by the time Asquith began to make earnest efforts to resolve the crisis, from the second half of 1913, it may already have been too late. On the other hand, Alvin Jackson, in *Home Rule*, argues that Asquith's 'masterly inactivity' brought the Home Rule crisis close to a settlement that would have been acceptable to a wide spectrum of opinion. However, one could still argue that Asquith ought to have been more proactive in addressing the challenge posed by the Ulster unionists.

Jalland argues strongly that when the Third Home Rule Bill was submitted to the House of Commons in April 1912 it should have allowed the four Protestant counties to opt out permanently. She argues that timely concessions on Ulster would have defused unionist opposition to the bill. She states that failure to do so was 'fatal'. Nicholas Mansergh, in *The Unresolved Question*, disagrees with her. He doubts whether the Ulster unionists, or the southern and British unionists, would have been satisfied with four counties. He points out too that Redmond and the IPP could not have surrendered part of Ulster in 1912 without serious electoral consequences. In his view, early appeasement of the Ulster unionists would have made little difference to the subsequent course of events. Jackson, in *Home Rule*, thinks that Jalland's case is stronger than Mansergh's. He reckons that some concessions on Ulster would have opened up divisions among the Ulster unionists, and between themselves and their Conservative and unionist allies. More importantly, it might have prevented the 'dangerous growth in Ulster unionist militancy'.

Andrew Bonar Law, as leader of the Conservative and Unionist Party, saw that the only way of keeping his deeply divided party united was to focus their attention on the Home Rule debate, so party strategy and personal commitment combined to ensure that the fight against Home Rule would top his agenda. In addition, Law's aggressive and emotive style added to the ferocity of the debate about Home Rule.

Conservatives and unionists condemned the Third Home Rule Bill as the product of a 'corrupt bargain' between the Liberals and Irish nationalists. In fact, there was wide support for Home Rule across the Liberal Party, right up to cabinet level, and in the Labour Party. Asquith justified the Third Home Rule Bill to Parliament on 11 April 1912 as the democratic wish of the overwhelming majority of the Irish people. He emphasised, though, 'The supreme power and authority of the imperial [British] parliament is to remain unimpaired and unchallenged.' He outlined the strict limits to be imposed on the new Irish government, and its continued subordination to the British Parliament and Crown.

County option

No special provision was made for Ulster, but the prime minister pointed out that unionist MPs outnumbered Home Rule MPs in Ulster by only 17 to 16. He stated, 'I have never underestimated the force...of the strong and determined hostility which is felt to Home Rule by the majority in the northeastern counties of Ulster.... But we cannot admit...the right of...a relatively small minority...to veto the verdict of the vast body of their countrymen.' Before the Third Home Rule Bill was drawn up, Augustine Birrell, the chief secretary for Ireland, wrote to Churchill, advocating the 'county option' formula whereby individual counties in Ulster could 'opt out' of Home Rule for a transitional period of 5 years. 'If this was done, there could be no civil war.' The 'county option' was rejected by a majority of the Liberal cabinet, but on 6 February 1912 Churchill and Lloyd George urged their colleagues to incorporate the 'county option' into the Third Home Rule Bill. Asquith informed George V of his government's willingness to provide 'some special treatment...for the Ulster counties', depending on the 'real extent and character of the Ulster resistance'.

Jalland sees the failure to include the 'county option' in the Home Rule Bill as a 'fatal' error. However, Asquith had no wish to alienate John Redmond and the IPP at a time when it was unclear whether significant concessions would be necessary, or effective. Asquith informed Redmond that the government would 'make such changes in the bill as fresh evidence of facts, or the pressure of British opinion, may render expedient'. However, he gave no indication that some key members of the Liberal cabinet were already advocating a 'county option'.

In June 1912 a Liberal backbencher, Thomas Agar-Robartes, a man with strong Protestant convictions, proposed an amendment to the Home Rule Bill whereby the four Ulster counties with a Protestant majority — Antrim, Down, Londonderry and Armagh — would be excluded from Home Rule. The Conservatives and unionists decided to support the amendment in an attempt to defeat the government. The amendment was defeated, but it is significant as the first public proposal for excluding some of Ulster from Home Rule. On 21 August 1912 Churchill wrote to Lloyd George declaring that 'the time has come for action about Ulster to be settled'. Lloyd George, however, suggested that it was better to wait for a proposal from the Ulster unionists than for the government to make such a divisive proposal itself. In a sense, he could see logic in Asquith's 'wait and see' strategy.

On 1 January 1913 Carson proposed a tactical amendment to the Third Home Rule Bill for the exclusion of all of Ulster. Asquith and most of his cabinet decided to reject the amendment outright, though Churchill and Lloyd George, and Birrell to a lesser extent, thought that the government should have responded by proposing the 'county option'. Patricia Jalland sees the Conservative and unionist support for the exclusion of Ulster from Home Rule as a tacit acknowledgement that they could not block Home Rule entirely and might have to settle for some degree of exclusion.

Asquith continued to 'wait and see' because he was not sure that the Conservatives and unionists, or the nationalists, were yet prepared to make concessions. However, the unionists strengthened their position while the waiting continued. The success of 'Ulster Day' in September 1912 was bolstered by a deluge of Ulster unionist propaganda across Great Britain. 'Ulster' became the main issue in British politics during the Home Rule Bill crisis.

Secret talks

Bonar Law and Churchill met at George V's residence at Balmoral on 18 September 1913 and exchanged views about Home Rule. Churchill was relieved to learn that the Conservative and Unionist leader was thinking about accepting Home Rule for most of Ireland once Ulster was excluded. Bonar Law subsequently informed Carson of his meeting and wrote that he had 'long thought' about a settlement that would allow southern Ireland to secure Home Rule as long as Ulster was excluded. Carson responded, 'On the whole things are shaping towards a desire to settle on terms of leaving "Ulster" out. A difficulty arises as to defining Ulster, and my own view is that the whole of Ulster should be excluded, but the minimum would be the six plantation counties.'

Asquith met Bonar Law in a series of secret meetings, on 14 October, 6 November and 10 December 1913, to see if an agreed settlement was possible. The prime minister insisted that Home Rule be granted soon and that nothing be done to create a permanent barrier to Irish unity. However, Asquith let Bonar Law know that a majority of the cabinet leaned towards a proposal by Lloyd George to exclude some Ulster counties for a limited number of years. Asquith spoke with Carson on 16 December and offered him 'Home Rule within Home Rule'. Carson was adamant in demanding that six counties be excluded permanently from Home Rule. That was rejected.

Jackson, having criticised Asquith's decision not to make concessions on Ulster in 1912, sees logic in his subsequent dealings. He points out that Asquith's secretive nature means there is no direct evidence of what he was thinking — it has to be inferred from scraps of evidence. However, by the start of 1914 the Ulster unionist leader and the Conservative and Unionist leader had conceded the case for Home Rule for most of Ireland. Disagreement was confined to 'Ulster': how many counties were to be excluded, and for how long.

Nationalist concessions

On 2 February 1914 Asquith met with Redmond and gave him the first clear indication that some form of exclusion was unavoidable. He subsequently wrote that Redmond 'shivered visibly and was a good deal perturbed'. It is difficult to explain how Redmond could have been so shocked at the announcement that some form of exclusion was necessary, given the clear drift of British public opinion. Following a meeting on 2 March 1914, Redmond, with Dillon, Devlin and O'Connor of the IPP, reluctantly agreed to a proposal for the exclusion of four counties, 'as the price of peace'. Under further pressure from Asquith, Redmond agreed to extend the period of exclusion to 5, and then 6, years. A general election would be held within the 6-year exclusion period, meaning that a Conservative and Unionist government could make exclusion permanent. Lloyd George was happy with the ambiguity inherent in a 6-year exclusion period — in effect it meant that exclusion would probably become permanent, but nationalists would not be asked to agree to permanent exclusion.

Unionist unwillingness to compromise

Asquith announced the government's intention in the Commons 1 week later, but Carson rejected the time limit, declaring, 'Ulster wants this question settled now and for ever. We do not want a sentence of death with a stay of execution for six years.' Jackson points out that Carson's intransigence angered several government ministers, including Churchill and Lloyd George. Churchill decided to take firm action to demonstrate the government's resolve to enforce the rule of law against unionist paramilitary threats, and to pre-empt a UVF conspiracy to seize weapons and munitions from British Army bases in Ulster. The briefing was bungled by the head of the British Army in Ireland. The resulting 'Curragh mutiny' on 20/21 March 1914 was highly embarrassing for the government. A public commitment had to be made not to deploy the British Army against the Ulster unionists. Jalland reckons that the 'mutiny' undermined the Home Rule policy more than any other single episode. Alan O'Day disagrees, but he recognises that the 'mutiny' strengthened Carson and the Ulster unionists significantly.

The landing of 35,000 rifles at Larne in April 1914 strengthened the UVF further. Maume writes of the Asquith government's response to the gun-running as being of 'the headless chicken variety'. Jalland sees the episode as adding to the British government's difficulties in dealing with the crisis. However, Maume and Jackson both play down the risk of armed rebellion by the Ulster unionists — they were still no match for the British Army, and violence would lose them support from the British public.

Buckingham Palace conference

On 25 May 1914 the Third Home Rule Bill won a large majority in the House of Commons. However, the government's amending bill, allowing individual counties to opt out of Home Rule for 6 years, was sabotaged in the House of Lords. George V suggested an all-party conference in Buckingham Palace. Between 21 and 24 July 1914 Asquith and Lloyd George (on behalf of the government party, together with Redmond and Dillon on behalf of Irish nationalists), negotiated with Bonar Law and

Lansdowne (on behalf of the Conservative Party, together with Carson and Craig on behalf of Ulster unionists).

The nationalists were prepared to concede the 'county option' for 6 years. However, Carson demanded that all nine counties in Ulster be excluded permanently. Bonar Law, with prior agreement from Carson, proposed that six counties be excluded. That was unacceptable to the government and the nationalists. Compromise proposals by the government to exclude the more Protestant parts of Fermanagh and Tyrone were rejected by both the nationalists and the Ulster unionists. The conference broke up without agreement. Two days later, on 26 July 1914, British soldiers killed four people and wounded 37 after a nationalist gun-smuggling operation at Howth, County Dublin. The contrast with the official collusion with the UVF gun-running at Larne made a great impression on Irish nationalists. On the other hand, Jackson reckons that Asquith was still confident that time was on his side.

Winners and losers

Events in Ireland were overtaken by the outbreak of the Great War on 4 August 1914. On that day Redmond appealed to Carson to agree to a fair settlement but, as Alan O'Day remarks, Carson was 'not in a compromising mood'. The government decided to take the initiative and the Government of Ireland Act (1914) received royal assent on 18 September 1914. Alvin Jackson, in *Ireland*, declares that Redmond had won 'a form of triumph' by the passing of the Government of Ireland Act. By contrast, he writes that the Ulster unionists were 'wounded by the enactment of Home Rule and the absence of any definite arrangement for the exclusion of Ulster'. In the House of Commons, after the final reading of the Home Rule Bill, some IPP MPs waved an Irish flag to celebrate their victory. The Conservatives and unionists had left the Commons in protest. It seemed to many that the Irish nationalists were the 'winners' and the Ulster unionists were the 'losers'. However, the reality was more complex.

The passing of the Government of Ireland Act, as the home rule bill became, seemed like a great achievement, but it was diminished by two provisos: the Act would not come into force until the Great War was over (and that took many more years than expected), and before it came into force 'special provision' would be made for Ulster. By the summer of 1914 Redmond had been forced to agree to four Ulster counties being excluded from Home Rule for 6 years. Jackson observes that Redmond's concessions 'damaged his credibility in Ireland, and not only with hardliners'. Yet Redmond's concessions were not enough to satisfy the Ulster unionists: they wanted six counties excluded permanently. Nationalists were upset at the likely prospect of partition, and most were worried that the unionists would secure permanent partition. David Fitzpatrick, in *Politics and Irish Life 1913–21: Provincial Experiences of War and Revolution*, finds that Royal Irish Constabulary reports showed there were no celebrations in Ireland on the passing of the Government of Ireland Act. Nationalists did not feel that they were 'winners'.

For Carson the Government of Ireland Act was a great disappointment. Like all the southern unionists, he had hoped to prevent any part of Ireland getting Home Rule. From late 1913, though, Carson had to accept political reality and come to terms with the fact that at most he might succeed in saving six Ulster counties from Home Rule. That compromise was a major defeat for southern unionists, and it worried the Ulster unionists in Donegal, Cavan and Monaghan also. Carson was angry that the Government of Ireland Act was passed without explicitly excluding six counties. Craig too was angry that the new law was enacted without defining the 'special provision' to be made for Ulster. Nonetheless, Craig and the Ulster unionists in the northeast were the real winners in the Third Home Rule Bill crisis. Back in 1910 Home Rule for all of Ireland had seemed inevitable, but thanks to the Ulster unionists' campaign some form of exclusion for part of Ulster was conceded by the Liberal government and by the IPP. The Buckingham Palace conference made it clear that the Ulster unionists could be confident of securing Counties Antrim and Londonderry, and most of Counties Down and Armagh, and at least parts of Tyrone and Fermanagh. The government and nationalists conceded the principle of exclusion for 6 years — but effectively that would have meant that partition would be permanent.

Political events, 1914–18

The Great War (1914–18) marked a watershed in modern Irish history. Before it, most Irish nationalists seemed content to accept a devolved Irish government within the UK. After it ended, most nationalists voted for Sinn Féin, a party committed to creating an independent Irish republic. Historians have focused much attention on the reasons for that dramatic transformation in nationalist politics.

What was the impact of the Great War on Irish politics?

On 3 August 1914, after news of Britain's impending involvement in the war was announced in the House of Commons, John Redmond, the IPP leader, pledged Ireland's support for Britain's war effort. It was a unilateral gesture that was well received by British MPs and it was instrumental, as Redmond hoped it would be, in persuading the Liberal government to pass the Government of Ireland Act in the following month. Edward Carson and James Craig also reacted quickly to the news of war by pledging unionists' support for the war effort. In fact, they went to Lord Kitchener, secretary of state for war, and offered to provide a division of trained soldiers from the UVF for the British Army. Those volunteers became the 36th (Ulster) Division. Redmond hesitated before committing the Irish Volunteers to front-line action until after the passing of the Government of Ireland Act. Then, on 20 September 1914, in a speech at Woodenbridge, County Wicklow, Redmond encouraged the Irish Volunteers to enlist in the British Army and fight in the war. Of the 170,000 men in the Irish Volunteers, only 12,000 opposed Redmond's call. The minority included most of the Volunteers' leadership and they kept the name 'Irish Volunteers'. The majority who supported Redmond became the 'National Volunteers'.

Redmond made his Woodenbridge speech for a number of reasons. Patrick Maume in *The Long Gestation* highlights Redmond's sense of moral obligation to Britain in return for Home Rule. He felt too that Britain's involvement in the war was justified as a response to German aggression, and he was sympathetic to 'little Belgium' following German atrocities committed there in the early days of the war. In addition, he believed that if unionists and nationalists fought side by side it would help to promote reconciliation and highlight the common ground they shared.

Historians have debated whether or not Redmond's decision to support Britain in the Great War was a mistake. Roy Foster, in *Modern Ireland*, writes that it was a 'disaster' for Redmond and the IPP because it tied them to an increasingly unpopular war. However, Joe Lee, in *Ireland 1912–1985*, reckons that Redmond had no choice, since he hoped to influence any postwar Irish settlement, especially with Ulster's 'special provision' yet to be defined. But the war cruelly exposed the limits of Redmond's achievement in September 1914: as Nicholas Mansergh points out in *The Unresolved Question*, Redmond had responsibility without power.

That was made very clear by Kitchener and the War Office. Redmond requested that the National Volunteers be organised into a distinct, Irish division in the British Army — as the Ulster Volunteer Force was organised into an 'Ulster Division' (with its own insignia). However, Kitchener prevented the formation of a distinctive Irish division, and Irish recruits were dispersed instead into existing Irish regiments in the British Army, or into British regiments. That publicly demonstrated Redmond's inability to influence government decisions, and it was widely seen as a reflection of the British establishment's continued favouritism towards the Ulster unionists. As the war dragged on, another problem emerged as fears of conscription grew. Stephen Gwynn, a friend and colleague of Redmond, credited the nationalist leader with blocking the extension of conscription to Ireland, but the issue still added to the IPP's difficulties by alienating young Irishmen.

Did Redmond's support for the war damage the IPP?

Historians have debated how much damage its support for the Great War caused the IPP. Paul Bew, in *Ideology and the Irish Question*, argues that it caused little damage and that the IPP's support held up very well until the aftermath of the 1916 Rising. However, Charles Townshend, in *Ireland: The 20th Century*, and Maume, in *The Long Gestation*, argue that the IPP was already running into trouble in 1915. Augustine Birrell, the chief secretary for Ireland, wrote that he felt that the situation in Ireland was one of 'actual menace' by late 1915.

Alvin Jackson, in *Home Rule*, suggests that the IPP might have been in a 'long decline' since the outbreak of the war. David Fitzpatrick's *Politics and Irish Life* shows that the number of meetings held by the IPP and its associated organisations, the Ancient

Order of Hibernians and the National Volunteers, dropped sharply in County Clare once the war started. Michael Wheatley, in *Nationalism and the Irish Party: Provincial Ireland 1910–1916*, finds the same pattern in the Irish midlands. Its support for the war, and its marginalisation after the formation of the wartime coalition government in May 1915, sapped support for the IPP. Bew, in *Ideology and the Irish Question*, and Alan O'Day, in *Irish Home Rule*, point to the IPP's success in elections held between 1914 and 1916 as evidence of its continued strength. However, Jackson reckons that the IPP's apparent strength simply reflected the absence of a credible challenge before 1917.

Why did the 1916 Rising occur?

Alvin Jackson, in *Home Rule*, writes that 'the Easter Rising is virtually unimaginable' without the First World War. Richard English in *Irish Freedom: A History of Nationalism in Ireland*, writes that the 1916 Rising was 'very much a World War I event', both in terms of the Rupert Brooke-style poetry of its leader, Patrick Pearse, and in terms of the opportunity it offered for a rebellion with a chance of success. The war did not cause the 1916 Rising, but it facilitated the pre-war ambitions of a clique in the Irish Republican Brotherhood (IRB) to stage a rebellion.

The Irish Republican Brotherhood

The IRB was a conspiratorial organisation committed to the establishment of an independent Irish republic. It was revived early in the new century by a veteran Fenian named Tom Clarke who recruited 'new blood', including Seán McDermott, Bulmer Hobson and Denis McCullough. Even before the outbreak of the Great War in August 1914, Clarke and McDermott were determined to launch a rebellion. Their central roles in the 1916 Rising are discussed by Michael Laffan in *The Resurrection of Ireland: The Sinn Féin Party 1916–1923* and Michael Foy and Brian Barton in *The Easter Rising*. Clarke, with McDermott and McCullough, formed the executive committee of the IRB from 1912 and, since McCullough was in Belfast, that meant that Clarke and McDermott virtually controlled the IRB.

Clarke and McDermott were almost alone inside the IRB in advocating a rising. They were a 'minority of a minority', as Roy Foster wrote. The IRB, with only 1,600 members in 1914, was not strong enough to stage a rising by itself. Members of the IRB had already infiltrated 'new nationalism' movements before the war, especially the GAA and the Gaelic League. F. S. L. Lyons, in *Culture and Anarchy in Ireland 1890–1939*, highlights how the Gaelic League provided a cultural inspiration for many of the men and women who later became militant nationalists. Nonetheless, a military force was needed to stage a credible rebellion.

'Carsonism'

Laffan, in *The Partition of Ireland*, identifies the formation of the UVF in 1913, and the success of unionist threats of violence in opposition to Home Rule, as instrumental in rekindling the 'Fenian flame'. Most historians, including George Boyce and Alvin Jackson, agree. Symptomatically, Patrick Pearse, a keen supporter of Home Rule as late as 1912, became an advocate of armed rebellion following the inspiration of the UVF. The Irish Volunteers, formed by Eóin Mac Néill in November 1913 in response to the challenge of the UVF, were recognised by Tom Clarke as an ideal instrument for staging his rebellion. The IRB infiltrated the Irish Volunteers' Committee from the start. Once Pearse, Joseph Plunkett and Thomas McDonagh, former Home Rulers, were sworn in to the IRB in late 1913, republicans made up half of the Irish Volunteers' ruling committee. Even before the war Clarke planned to use the Irish Volunteers to fight his rebellion against Britain.

Nonetheless, until the Great War the vast majority of the Irish Volunteers, like nationalists generally, were still committed to the IPP and its Home Rule agenda. The outbreak of the Great War helped Clarke and McDermott to turn their determination to stage a rising into a reality. 'England's difficulty' was seen as 'Ireland's opportunity'. Britain's distraction in the war, and the possibility of securing support from Germany, made a successful rebellion 'just about conceivable'. Yet the IRB president, McCullough, and most other members of the IRB thought it best to avoid a premature military confrontation with Britain. Laffan, in *The Resurrection of Ireland*, shows that it was not until early in 1916 that Clarke persuaded the supreme council of the IRB to agree to staging a rebellion at some time in the future — but even then he never told them about the rebellion he had planned for Easter of that year. As Jackson observes in *Home Rule*, Clarke and McDermott were prepared to 'subvert' the constitution of the IRB in order to stage their rebellion.

The 'Sinn Féin' Volunteers

The split in the Irish Volunteers about whether or not to support Britain in the Great War in 1914 left the IRB with greater influence over the 12,000 anti-war Volunteers (increasingly called the 'Sinn Féin' Volunteers because of Sinn Féin's anti-war stance). In that respect the war provided the IRB conspirators with both the opportunity to rebel, and a paramilitary body that Clarke's clique could manipulate for its own ends. No less importantly, the disillusionment that was increasingly felt with the IPP during the Great War meant that the men and women who were, in Roy Foster's phrase, 'pitch-forked into action with no notice whatsoever' in Dublin in Easter 1916 were willing to fight for Irish freedom in a way that would have been unimaginable before the Great War began.

In May 1915 the IRB executive (essentially Clarke and McDermott) appointed a military committee to draw up the detailed plans for the rebellion. Clarke and McDermott joined those men to form the military council in September 1915. Russell Rees, in *Ireland 1905–25*, argues that the establishment of the military council was the 'single most important factor in the planning of the Easter Rising'. Clarke's plans were boosted in January 1916 when, having learned of James Connolly's intention to launch a Marxist rebellion against British rule, he persuaded Connolly to include the Irish Citizen Army, a force of about 200, in the IRB rebellion.

Clarke did not expect to free Ireland of British rule in his own lifetime. Yet he was anxious that his rising should be sufficiently credible to inspire a new generation of Irish nationalists. Roger Casement, on behalf of the IRB military council, travelled to Germany in the hope of establishing an Irish Brigade from among the Irish prisoners of war to fight for Ireland. That mission failed, but 20,000 guns were shipped to the rebels by the Germans. Casement and the guns were intercepted, however, just before the rising. With no chance then that a rising could succeed, Eóin Mac Néill, the Irish Volunteers leader, countermanded an earlier order for the Volunteers to 'parade' on Easter Sunday 1916. Clarke and his clique decided to proceed with the rising on Easter Monday anyway. Without the necessary manpower or guns to succeed, it was to be a 'blood sacrifice'.

It is difficult to explain the concept of a 'blood sacrifice', but essentially it was a romantic idea that someone's death would win God's favour for a cause, rather like the Christian belief that Jesus' death brought blessings to humankind. The 1916 Rising was planned for Easter Sunday to make clear the idea that the men who died for Ireland were engaged in a 'blood sacrifice' for their country. The date was also chosen to symbolise Ireland's 'resurrection' from British oppression. It was not a notion peculiar to Irish nationalists at that time — young men from all across Europe were being persuaded of the efficacy of their dying for their countries during the Great War.

A rising of intellectuals?

F. X. Martin, in 'The Evolution of a Myth: The Easter Rising, Dublin 1916' (in *Nationalism: The Nature and Evolution of an Idea*, ed. E. Kamenka), suggests that the 1916 Rising was 'a revolution of the intellectuals', as in the manner of the 1848 revolutions across Europe. Three of the seven signatories of the 1916 Rising proclamation were poets, while James Connolly was a Marxist intellectual of international repute.

The man who was officially at the head of the 1916 Rising, and who read the proclamation at the General Post Office in Dublin, was Patrick Pearse. He was a poet and educationalist who was greatly inspired by the 'new nationalism'. Lyons, in *Culture and Anarchy in Ireland*, identifies him as one of the many members of the Gaelic League who later became militant nationalists. Thomas McDonagh was another poet inspired by the 'new nationalism', as was Joseph Plunkett. In fact, the first in-depth report on the 1916 Rising in the *New York Times* called the rising a 'revolution of the poets'. Ireland's greatest poet of the time, W. B. Yeats, in his poem 'Easter, 1916', wondered whether the rebels had been inspired by his own literary efforts. F. X. Martin makes the point too that the 1916 Rising was 'staged' like a play, and he points out that Pearse, McDonagh and Plunkett had all staged plays of their own. Richard English, in *Irish Freedom*, endorses the idea that there was a definite 'poetic-intellectual element' to the 1916 Rising. Arguably, Connolly was the greatest intellectual among the 1916 rebels, and his Marxist writings enjoyed an international reputation, but under Pearse's influence he adopted the romantic idea of a 'blood sacrifice' to justify an armed rebellion even when its chances of military success were minimal.

Nonetheless, there is a very strong case to be made that the 1916 Rising was not really 'a revolution of the intellectuals'. Ruth Dudley Edwards, in her biography *Patrick Pearse: The Triumph of Failure*, emphasises Pearse's personal limitations. He wrote a great deal about his ideas, and that is a key reason why he made such an impression on historians, but he was only a 'front man' for the real mastermind behind the rising — IRB veteran Tom Clarke. It was Clarke and McDermott who recruited Pearse, McDonagh and Plunkett into the IRB in late 1913 in order to get control over the Irish Volunteers' ruling committee. Clarke recognised that the young intellectuals could be useful for his plans. Pearse's romantic idealism, which was obvious in his speeches and writings, made him the perfect 'front man' in a rising intended to inspire a new generation of Irish separatists. Pearse's speech at the grave of O'Donovan Rossa in 1915 was made on Clarke's invitation. Laffan accepts Mrs Clarke's evidence to the effect that Clarke was the 'real' president of the republic declared on Easter Monday. Clarke's name was the first signatory to the 1916 Proclamation, while there is a lot of evidence that Connolly was the effective commander-in-chief of the rebels during Easter week, not the poetic Pearse.

How did Sinn Féin replace the IPP as the voice of nationalist Ireland?

Historians, including Michael Laffan in *The Partition of Ireland* and Alvin Jackson in *Home Rule*, generally agree that British government actions served to undermine the constitutionalist stance of the IPP in the period 1914–18 and helped to radicalise nationalist opinion, especially in the aftermath of the 1916 Rising. The rise of Sinn Féin owed much to the party's ability to capitalise on the radicalisation of nationalists and harness it. It also depended on the failure of the IPP to maintain its previous monopoly of nationalists' support.

Problems facing the IPP

Jackson, in *Home Rule*, reminds us what an important achievement the Government of Ireland Act (1914) was. However, the provisos that it was not to be implemented until the Great War had ended, and the 'special provision' promised for Ulster, created problems for the IPP. The Ulster unionists' threats of violence were seen to have paid off. According to Laffan, in *The Partition of Ireland*, 'Carsonism' had undermined Redmond's constitutionalist stance and rekindled the 'Fenian flame'. The formation of the Irish Volunteers under Eóin Mac Néill in November 1913 was a sign that many nationalists were losing confidence in Redmond and in parliamentary politics.

Historians are agreed that the suspension of the Government of Ireland Act (1914) put Redmond in the difficult position of having responsibility but no power.

Yet Mansergh, in *The Unresolved Question*, argues that Redmond should have demanded power and should have considered setting up a provisional government to secure it. Nonetheless, Redmond still enjoyed enough authority to win the support of the vast majority of the Irish Volunteers for his pro-British stance at Woodenbridge in September 1914. Paul Bew, in *Ideology and the Irish Question*, and Alan O'Day, in *Irish Home Rule*, argue that the IPP's support held up very well until the aftermath of the 1916 Rising. On the other hand, Charles Townshend, in *Ireland: The 20th Century*, Patrick Maume, in *The Long Gestation*, and Alvin Jackson, in *Home Rule*, argue that the IPP began to lose more and more support as the Great War turned out to be a bloodier and longer conflict than expected. Fitzpatrick's *Politics and Irish Life* and Wheatley's *Nationalism and the Irish Party* highlight evidence of the IPP's decline before the 1916 Rising.

Redmond's declaration of support for Britain at Woodenbridge opened the way for Sinn Féin, a small anti-war party, to gain prominence. It also split the Irish Volunteers, leaving a 'rump' of Volunteers who were deeply infiltrated by the IRB. On the other hand, Redmond's gesture was not reciprocated by the British government, and Kitchener and the War Office humiliated him more than once. The growing threat of conscription alienated many young men as the war dragged on.

Redmond's decision not to accept a cabinet post in the coalition government formed in 1915 has been widely questioned by historians, including Laffan and Jackson. It left the IPP marginalised at Westminster. Jackson blames Redmond for what he considers a tactical error, but he criticises the British government too for promoting Carson in Redmond's absence. The actions of the British government from 1914 undermined the IPP, but it is clear that Redmond must share some of the blame for his increasingly weak position.

The government's response to the 1916 Rising

Redmond condemned the 1916 Rising soon after it began. However, he was out of touch with the change in mood among nationalists caused by the executions (their number and manner). John Dillon, deputy leader of the IPP, reflected the ambiguity of nationalist sentiment when he condemned the rising in the House of Commons in May 1916 but expressed empathy for the patriotism of the rebels. The British government's decision to allow three more executions after Dillon's appeal for it to stop the killings was generally seen as yet another snub to the IPP and underlined its weakness.

The post-Rising imposition of martial law, with thousands of house searches, arrests, internment and other forms of military harassment, was a 'major error' according to Eunan O'Halpin in *The Decline of the Union: British Government in Ireland, 1892–1920*. Government policy, without meaning to, hammered home the message that the IPP was powerless. David Lloyd George's double-dealings with Redmond and Carson in July 1916, regarding the 'temporary' nature of partition in a government-backed settlement proposal, caused 'fatal' damage to the IPP, according to Stephen Gwynn,

Redmond's friend and biographer. Dillon thought the same at the time. Laffan agrees that it 'severely damaged' the IPP.

The transformation of Sinn Féin

Until 1916 Sinn Féin was a marginal group which advocated a Hungarian-style 'dual monarchy' for Ireland. Its opposition to the Great War brought it prominence — but no electoral success. However, the British authorities helped to transform Sinn Féin into a major republican movement by mistakenly associating it with the 1916 Rising. Arthur Griffith and other Sinn Féin activists were interned along with republicans, and that act unwittingly created a cohesive revolutionary elite, according to Jackson in *Home Rule*. Lloyd George, newly appointed prime minister in place of Asquith, freed Sinn Féin members and Volunteers from internment as a goodwill gesture in December 1916 ahead of the Convention planned to address the 'Irish Question'. However, that simply strengthened the radicals.

By-election results in Ireland in 1917 showed, in Jackson's words, 'no avalanche-like collapse' in the IPP. The party put up a creditable performance against the republican candidate, Count George Plunkett, in North Roscommon, and Dillon reckoned that it might have won the South Longford by-election but for the intervention of Archbishop Walsh of Dublin, who condemned the IPP's concessions to the Ulster unionists. Nonetheless, Laffan points out that Sinn Féin's victories gained it momentum and united advanced nationalist opinion behind it. With its central office, clubs and two newspapers, it provided an organisation to harness the growing radicalisation. It also had the Sinn Féin name, which the British authorities had wrongly associated with the 1916 Rising. Sinn Féin had 11,000 members in July 1917, and 200,000 by October 1917. Sinn Féin's ability to harness the growing alienation of nationalists was critical in ensuring its successes.

Lloyd George tried to weaken support for republicanism by releasing some of the leading rebels — including Éamon de Valera and Thomas Ashe. However, their freedom boosted the radicals further. In July 1917 de Valera won a massive majority for Sinn Féin in the East Clare by-election. The British government responded by arresting the most outspoken republicans. One of them, Ashe, went on hunger strike in September 1917 and died while being force-fed. His funeral attracted an enormous crowd in Dublin. Government actions, whether conciliatory or coercive, unwittingly gave extra momentum to Sinn Féin.

Sinn Féin boycotted the Irish Convention that opened in July 1917. Its failure, which Jackson reckons was not because of Ulster unionist intransigence, as is generally assumed, but because of the incompetence of its chairman, undermined further the IPP's diminishing credibility. It underlined the apparent futility of old-style politics.

The success of Sinn Féin cannot be ascribed entirely to the often ham-fisted actions of the British government. In October 1917 de Valera, president of the Irish Volunteers, became the president of Sinn Féin also. He was an austere yet charismatic leader. He framed a new constitution for Sinn Féin, designed to hold together both constitutionalists and more militant Volunteers who demanded a republic. De Valera's personal appeal contrasted with that of Redmond, who was demoralised and falling into ill-health.

Early in 1918 Sinn Féin suffered three electoral setbacks: in South Armagh and East Tyrone in Ulster (where nationalists were afraid of splitting the nationalist vote), and in Waterford (where Redmond's brother won his seat after his death). These results gave hope to the IPP under its new leader, Dillon, and undermined Sinn Féin's confidence. However, in April 1918 the British government decided to extend conscription to Ireland. Diarmaid Ferriter, in *The Transformation of Ireland*, shows that Irish Volunteer numbers surged in response. The British government backed down in the face of general opposition in Ireland, from Sinn Féin, the IPP and the Catholic Church — but Richard English, in *Irish Freedom*, concludes that the conscription crisis 'guaranteed the success of Sinn Féin' in the forthcoming election.

As if to galvanise Sinn Féin further, the British authorities arrested 73 of its leading members in the so-called 'German plot' in May 1918. Nationalist sentiment was shown in a by-election in Cavan which Griffith, the founder of Sinn Féin, won with a great majority. The British government responded in turn with an army crackdown on Sinn Féin, the Irish Volunteers and GAA clubs, and by 'proclaiming' counties, thereby arousing ever stronger nationalist opposition.

Lloyd George called a general election after the Great War ended. Republicans threw themselves into the campaign with vigour. Sinn Féin offered the electorate a Four Point Plan, calling for the establishment of an Irish constituent assembly, abstention from Westminster and withholding consent to British rule, and an appeal to the postwar Peace Conference for 'national self-determination'. The programme seemed a plausible means of achieving Irish independence by peaceful means. Sinn Féin won a landslide victory, with 73 MPs elected.

A significant factor in Sinn Féin's success was the weakness of the IPP. In more than 20 constituencies there was no IPP candidate. Dillon himself admitted afterwards to T. P. O'Connor, the IPP MP for Liverpool, that his party organisation could not compare to that of Sinn Féin. The IPP offered voters nothing very new — 'dominion home rule' — but appealed mainly on the basis of its past achievements and a fear of Sinn Féin radicalism. Maume, in *The Long Gestation*, shows that the IPP vote held up fairly well among older people, but Sinn Féin captured the votes of the young, and the IPP was virtually wiped out.

The actions of the British government helped to undermine the IPP, yet much of the blame for its collapse must be attributed to the failings of the party leadership to respond effectively to the challenges posed by the Ulster unionists, by the British government's repeated mishandling of nationalist opinion both before but especially after the 1916 Rising, and by the competition offered by Sinn Féin. On the other hand, Sinn Féin under Griffith and then de Valera succeeded in harnessing the growing alienation from the British government and from the IPP, and in channelling the enthusiasm of enough nationalists to win a landslide victory in the 1918 general election.

Events in Ireland, 1919–25

Sinn Féin's landslide victory in the general election of December 1918 gave it a mandate from nationalist Ireland to establish an independent Irish republic. However, the British government did not allow itself to be displaced without a struggle and, despite an increasingly violent campaign, the Irish Republican Army (IRA) was not able to drive the British Army from Ireland. By the middle of 1921 Sinn Féin and the British government both recognised the need for a compromise settlement. From June 1921 six Ulster counties were governed by a 'Home Rule' administration in Belfast, while the other 26 counties left the UK and formed the Irish Free State in 1922. It was a settlement that provoked widespread opposition within Northern Ireland, and a civil war across the border. It was not until the end of 1925 that the settlement took on an air of permanence.

How was the Anglo–Irish War fought?

Dáil Éireann

All of the Irish MPs elected in the general election of December 1918 were invited to attend an Irish parliament, Dáil Éireann, established on 21 January 1919. Only 27 Sinn Féin MPs attended the first Dáil; 34 other Sinn Féin MPs were imprisoned at the time. The 26 unionist MPs for Ireland and the six IPP MPs refused to attend. The Declaration of Independence was read in the Dáil, associating that body with the 1916 proclamation. A provisional constitution was approved, with a provisional government to comprise a prime minister and four other ministers. A 'Democratic Programme' was endorsed, promising vague economic and social reforms. The Dáil nominated a team of negotiators comprising de Valera, Griffith and Plunkett, to take Ireland's claim for national self-determination to the Paris Peace Conference.

The Dáil met again on 1 April 1919, with 52 MPs in attendance. Éamon de Valera, the president of Sinn Féin, had recently been sprung from Lincoln Prison by Michael Collins and Harry Boland, both senior IRB figures. He was elected as the Irish prime minister by the Dáil, but soon came to be called the 'President of the Irish Republic'. Collins was elected as the minister for finance. Arthur Griffith became the minister for home affairs. Cathal Brugha was the minister for defence, with charge of the Irish Volunteers (which became the Irish Republican Army). George Plunkett, William Cosgrave, Eóin Mac Néill and Countess Markievicz, a leading survivor of James Connolly's Irish Citizen Army and the first woman ever to be elected as an MP in the UK, were also appointed to the Sinn Féin cabinet.

Sinn Féin tried to create a viable Irish government to displace the British government peacefully from Ireland. Recent scholarship by Tom Garvin, Arthur Mitchell and others has stressed the achievements of the Dáil government in the areas of local government and justice. Cosgrave's Department of Local Government had its authority recognised by 27 of the 33 county councils in Ireland. A network of

Sinn Féin courts operated effectively with popular support over much of Ireland from June 1919 to August 1920, after which the British government deliberately hampered their activities.

To make an Irish government viable, money had to be raised. Collins took responsibility for raising £500,000 — half of it in Ireland and half from the USA. A short film was commissioned to help raise the money, which was shown in cinemas across Ireland. The Dáil's authority was recognised by all but four of the county councils across Ireland. However, the British administration in Dublin Castle did not 'wither away' peacefully as anticipated. That confirmed some republican militants in their view that an armed struggle would be required to win Irish freedom.

Sinn Féin naively thought that the American president, Woodrow Wilson, who made a speech in favour of 'national self-determination', would support its claim for Irish independence. In fact, the American president looked on Britain's prime minister, David Lloyd George, as his main ally in the world. The Sinn Féin delegation was ignored at Paris. Their failure to have Ireland's case considered at the Peace Conference was a major setback for the constitutionalists in the republican movement, while it strengthened the position of its more militant elements. The suppression of the Dáil by the British government in September 1919 weakened the constitutional wing of the republican movement further.

Irish Republican Army

Cathal Brugha, as the Dáil's minister for defence, was officially in charge of the army of the Irish republic, the IRA. However, Brugha found it very difficult to control the various IRA units in the provinces in the face of British hostility. Richard Mulcahy, head of the IRA's general headquarters staff in Dublin, was an IRB member loyal to Michael Collins, president of the IRB. Collins himself was the director of operations in the IRA. Brugha resented Collins' influence over the IRA — and that resentment had major consequences during the subsequent civil war.

The Anglo–Irish War, or War of Independence as it is often called, started with an incident at Soloheadbeg, County Tipperary, in January 1919, when two Royal Irish Constabulary (RIC) officers were killed by the Third Tipperary Brigade of the IRA, who wanted to take their guns and the explosives the police were escorting. This action was not authorised by the IRA GHQ, as the politicians in Sinn Féin were worried about losing public support through the use of violence. The GHQ gave retrospective sanction to the violence in *An tÓglach* at the end of January, declaring that Ireland was in a 'state of war' and that warfare with the forces of the British Crown was legitimate. In reality, however, the initiative in the Anglo–Irish War lay with local commanders.

Charles Townshend, in *Political Violence in Ireland: Government and Resistance Since 1848*, identifies three main phases in the Anglo–Irish War. Until January 1920 the IRA launched small-scale attacks on the RIC. In 1919 there were 18 police officers killed — in small numbers, in a number of different places. Collins' 'Squad' assassinated several of the Dublin Metropolitan Police's detectives, in G Division, who specialised in gathering intelligence on republicans. In such counter-intelligence operations Collins was helped by sympathisers in the police such as Éamon Broy.

Peter Hart, in *The IRA at War 1916–1923*, argues that the IRA's guerrilla war did not start in earnest until it was authorised by the GHQ in January 1920. From early 1920 the IRA grew more ambitious, attacking and destroying 16 occupied RIC barracks by summer. From late summer IRA 'flying columns', involving large numbers of IRA volunteers coming together for specific operations, began to function. These men were full-time soldiers, living away from home, able to fight over large areas. Richard English observes that 'these were the people who drove the war'. At Kilmichael in County Cork an IRA flying column killed 18 Auxiliary police officers.

The geography of the war

Peter Hart, in *The IRA at War*, examines the geography of the violence. He shows that Cork city and county ('Rebel Cork') were at the centre of the IRA campaign. There were significant if lesser numbers of IRA actions in Cork's neighbouring counties — Tipperary, Clare, Limerick and Kerry — and also in Dublin city. Beyond Dublin and the south, only counties Cavan and Monaghan featured at all in the war.

In trying to explain the geography of the war, Hart shows that the IRA in certain localities took the initiative and provoked responses by the Crown's forces which generated a wider feeling of resentment in the nationalist community — which in turn resulted in more support for the IRA. Each attack on the Crown's forces resulted in increased activity by the RIC and, increasingly, by the British Army. Curfews were imposed, fairs and markets were disrupted, houses were searched and whole counties were put under military rule. More and more of the public were affected by security force measures, which in turn worsened a sense of oppression that further strengthened support for the IRA. The violence took on a 'tit-for-tat' character that fuelled its escalation.

The IRA volunteers

Historians have tried to define the type of person most likely to join the IRA, but have discovered no clear social profile. Tom Garvin, in *The Evolution of Irish Nationalist Politics*, suggests that IRA members tended to come disproportionately from 'lower middle-class' families in small towns or farms. Joost Augusteijn, in *From Public Defiance to Guerrilla Warfare: The Experience of Ordinary Volunteers in the Irish War of Independence 1916–1921*, also emphasises the 'middling' background of rural IRA members. Hart, in *The IRA at War*, tests the correlation between IRA membership and membership of Sinn Féin, the GAA and the Gaelic League and finds that it was weak. The one factor that showed a strong correlation was a Christian Brothers education: the brothers' 'faith and fatherland' teaching seems to have influenced many young men in a revolutionary direction. IRA members generally seem to have been well educated. Alvin Jackson, in *Ireland*, observes that former service with the British Army 'also appears as a common characteristic of the IRA'.

British policy

The British response to IRA violence in 1919 was poorly conceived. Jackson, in *Ireland*, states that the British government was distracted from Irish affairs by having to deal with the aftermath of the Great War across Europe, the problems posed by demobilisation and economic reconstruction at home, and the growth of labour unrest. There was a 'growing British desire for disengagement' from Irish affairs, but Lloyd George's postwar coalition government was divided on how to manage that disengagement. Townshend, in his analysis of the British campaign in Ireland, criticises the failure of the British government to define its political objectives in Ireland, resulting in a political vacuum.

As the IRA campaign slowly escalated in 1919, the British government preferred to see it as a 'law and order' problem created by 'murder gangs' and failed to address its underlying causes. Yet the IRA campaign, massively boosted by the nationalist boycott of the RIC promoted by Sinn Féin, led to a sharp fall in morale among the police, who were mostly Catholic and mildly nationalist themselves. The number of officers resigning from the RIC grew, while the number of recruits fell sharply. Unwilling to admit that the 'Troubles' were any more than a policing matter, the British government authorised the strengthening of the RIC from February 1920 by employing British soldiers who had been demobilised after the Great War as police officers in Ireland. Those men, in their distinctive black and khaki uniforms, were dubbed the 'Black and Tans'. They were not trained as policemen, and they did not behave as such. From July 1920 the RIC was strengthened with an Auxiliary division of policemen consisting of demobilised British Army officers. Jackson reckons they were 'probably the least disciplined of the Crown's forces', given to drunkenness and occasional brutality as well as reckless bravery.

As the violence grew in 1920, Major General Henry Tudor, the police chief, and some of his political masters, including Prime Minister Lloyd George, sanctioned an unofficial policy of 'reprisals'. For example, when an RIC officer was killed in Balbriggan, near Dublin, in September 1920, police destroyed 50 homes in the village, and two civilians were killed. When Collins' 'Squad' killed 14 British intelligence officers on 'Bloody Sunday' in November 1920, Auxiliary police officers opened fire on a crowd of spectators at a GAA football match at Croke Park in Dublin, killing 12 people and wounding dozens of others. Elsewhere three prisoners (two IRA members and another, Conor Clune, who was not involved) were shot, allegedly while trying to escape. In December 1920, Auxiliaries burnt the city hall and library in Cork, and most of the city's largest department stores, in reprisal for attacks on their members.

Russell Rees, in *Ireland 1905–25*, points out that the Crown forces' campaign of counter-terror served to increase nationalists' sense of being oppressed, while also turning British public opinion against the government's policy in Ireland. Rees notes that 'the sheer brutality of "Bloody Sunday" shocked opinion in Ireland and Britain'. Diarmaid Ferriter, in *The Transformation of Ireland*, highlights the success and effectiveness of Sinn Féin's publicity machine in exposing the 'reprisals' policy through the *Irish Bulletin*, which was widely circulated in Britain as well as Ireland. The British resort to counter-terror proved to be a decisive tactical error.

The Government of Ireland Act (1920)

Jackson, in *Ireland*, remarks that 'it was not just that the IRA was shooting its way into the purview of the British cabinet'; the end of the Great War raised the issue of the Government of Ireland Act (1914), which was supposed to come into operation once the war had ended. Belatedly, in September 1919 Prime Minister Lloyd George established the Long Committee to give shape to his Irish policy. Walter Long had been Carson's predecessor as leader of the Irish unionists. Rees points out that Long's sympathies, and the power of the Conservatives in Lloyd George's coalition government, guaranteed a settlement that was favourable to the Ulster unionists.

O'Leary and Maume, in *Controversial Issues in Anglo–Irish Relations*, among others, have shown how James Craig, the leading Ulster unionist, used his influence in the coalition government, of which he was a member, to shape the Government of Ireland Act (1920) to his liking. John Kendle, in his biography of Long, shows that his committee wanted to keep all of Ireland within the UK by facilitating Irish unity through a strong Council of Ireland. This would be designed to foster cooperation between the devolved governments proposed for a Southern Ireland comprising the three southern provinces, and a Northern Ireland comprising all of Ulster. A nine-county Northern Ireland would have had a Catholic minority of about 46%, and the two communities would have been forced to work together in some kind of harmony. Craig, however, with Balfour's support, made sure that the Council of Ireland would be powerless, and he secured a six-county Northern Ireland — the largest area in which he could be confident of having supremacy over northern Catholics, according to Joe Lee in *Ireland 1912–1985*. James Craig's brother, Charles Craig, told the House of Commons that the Ulster unionists saw a six-county Northern Ireland as a guarantee of their 'absolute security'. On 27 May 1920 Craig won the endorsement of the Ulster Unionist Council in favour of the Government of Ireland Act (1920), with only 80 votes against it out of 390.

Why were both sides willing to agree to a truce in July 1921?

Determining the strengths and weaknesses of the IRA at the time of the truce is difficult because, as Roy Foster observes in *Modern Ireland*, those who supported the Anglo–Irish Treaty and those who opposed it both had 'a vested interest' in emphasising either the IRA's weaknesses or its strengths respectively. When arguing in favour of the treaty in the Dáil, Kevin O'Higgins, assistant minister for local government, stated that 'there would be no question of military victory' by the IRA if the war had continued. Yet Richard English, in *Irish Freedom*, concludes that 'the IRA had considerable success in thwarting British rule in 1919–21...the IRA could not simply be defeated'. Townshend's verdict is that the IRA's achievement was 'to find that by matching its operations to its means, it could ensure its survival for long enough to achieve psychological victory out of military stalemate'. All historians are agreed that the Anglo–Irish War had reached a stalemate by the summer of 1921.

In March 1921 the IRA's GHQ in Dublin was raided by the British Army, a good indication of the improved intelligence the Crown's forces were gathering. By April 1921 the Sinn Féin courts had been, in Jackson's words, 'thoroughly crushed'. The IRA suffered a tremendous setback in Dublin with the Customs House debacle in May 1921, with 70 volunteers killed or captured by British soldiers. In fact, by that date 5,500 IRA volunteers were imprisoned out of a total strength of perhaps 7,500. In addition, there continued to be major difficulties in securing weapons: English quotes an IRA leader from County Longford stating, 'Even at the best of times we had arms for only a fraction of the men available.' Yet, while their colleagues in Dublin were under severe pressure by the summer of 1921, the IRA in Cork and Tipperary was confident that it could sustain the war for years into the future. Hart, in *The IRA at War*, points to a new development whereby the IRA had begun to acquire and use explosives effectively. A bomb at Youghal in County Cork inflicted 29 casualties on the British Army in early summer 1921 — 'the bloodiest single ambush of the entire campaign'. Hart declares, 'Here lay the real future of guerrilla warfare in Ireland.'

The work of English and Hart suggests that Michael Collins was unduly pessimistic when he told the chief secretary for Ireland, Hamar Greenwood, 'We could not have lasted another three weeks.' Yet Collins probably judged correctly that the military balance was shifting in favour of the British in the summer of 1921, and that the republicans' bargaining position might grow weaker in the future.

As late as May 1921 the British government was still committed to enforcing the Government of Ireland Act (1920), and the cabinet voted against a Liberal suggestion that peace talks might be held with Sinn Féin. When Sinn Féin boycotted the parliament established for 'Southern Ireland', the British cabinet responded on 2 June 1921 with a decision to impose martial law on all of Southern Ireland from 14 July. Neville Macready, the head of the British Army in Ireland, was asked to prepare for such a course. However, Macready warned the British government that his soldiers were suffering from psychological fatigue, and indicated that he would need many additional soldiers. Indeed, the possibility was discussed of drafting in 250,000 soldiers. Macready also demanded the right to execute Sinn Féin leaders at will, including Éamon de Valera and Arthur Griffith. His attitude was 'all out, or get out'. Nicholas Mansergh, in *The Unresolved Question*, reckons that such draconian measures seemed excessive even to diehard Conservatives, and persuaded them of the need for some kind of compromise.

Hart, in *The IRA at War*, and English, in *Radicals and the Republic: Socialist Republicanism in the Irish Free State 1927–1937*, have shown that the IRA had forced the British Army to a military stalemate. Ferriter too concludes that the IRA was close to achieving a military stalemate, and had won a propaganda victory against the British by the summer of 1921.

Graham Walker, in *A History of the Ulster Unionist Party: Protest, Pragmatism and Pessimism*, states that the implementation of the Government of Ireland Act (1920) was delayed by Lloyd George while efforts were made to 'settle' the south. All historians of the period, including Walker and Alvin Jackson, are agreed that Craig was anxious to consolidate the northern state as soon as possible, because he did not entirely trust British politicians not to make concessions on partition in order to secure a deal with Sinn Féin.

On the other hand, Alan O'Day, in *Irish Home Rule*, points out that from the British government's perspective, negotiations with Sinn Féin only became a feasible option after the establishment of Northern Ireland in June 1921. With the Ulster unionists 'sorted', the government could focus its attention on the southern nationalists. It was by then clear to British politicians that there could be no military solution. Sir John Anderson, a senior civil servant in Dublin Castle, warned the government in June 1921 that to escalate the military campaign in Ireland would be the 'wildest folly'. The British policy of reprisals was widely condemned in Britain by churchmen, politicians from all parties, the press and even some members of the cabinet. The South African leader, General Jan Smuts, warned Lloyd George that British policy in Ireland was a 'calamity' and was undermining Britain's prestige and moral authority in the dominions and in the USA. Lloyd George was particularly worried about American opinion.

Peace moves

George Boyce, in *Englishmen and Irish Troubles: British Public Opinion and the Making of Irish Policy, 1918–1922*, and Francis Costello, in *The Irish Revolution and its Aftermath 1916–1923*, both agree with earlier historians that Smuts was instrumental in persuading Lloyd George to consider a peaceful strategy on Ireland. Smuts helped to draft George V's conciliatory speech for the opening of the Belfast parliament on 22 June 1921, although Costello shows that the British cabinet was also involved in the drafting. It was the positive reception to the speech in the Irish and British press that encouraged Lloyd George to gamble on talks with Sinn Féin. Under Smuts' influence, Lloyd George got his cabinet's approval for an offer of dominion status. Roy Foster emphasises that the Conservative agenda on crown, empire, security and Ulster allowed Lloyd George little room for manoeuvre.

Why did the Anglo–Irish Treaty of 1921 provoke a civil war?

De Valera had four meetings with Lloyd George in London in July 1921. He rejected the British offer of dominion status. De Valera's decision not to engage in further peace talks has puzzled historians. Tim Pat Coogan, in his biographies of both de Valera and Michael Collins, states that de Valera knew that a republic was not achievable and so decided to let Collins, who came to be seen as the real leader of nationalist Ireland during de Valera's 18-month stay in the USA, take the blame for the compromise that would be necessary with the British. Costello, who is more objective than Coogan, does not altogether disagree. Certainly Collins did not want to lead the Irish delegation to negotiate the treaty in London, and he told the IRB Supreme Council that he went because those who ought to have gone did not have the courage to make the hard decisions that would be required.

Collins, as president of the IRB, director of intelligence in the IRA and finance minister in the Dáil executive, understood the military situation far better than de Valera. Collins knew that the IRA, with around 2,500 volunteers active against 40,000 British soldiers backed by 17,000 members of the RIC, Black and Tans and Auxiliaries, and with a crippling lack of guns and munitions, could not deliver a 'knock-out blow' against the British. By 6 December 1921 Collins was clear that the Sinn Féin delegates could not secure a better deal from the British, and he knew that the resumption of the IRA campaign would not strengthen their bargaining position. Cathal Brugha, the Dáil's minister for defence, produced an inventory of the IRA's weapons in December 1921 that showed clearly how very small an arsenal it possessed. The Sinn Féin delegates took a pragmatic decision to sign the treaty. Prophetically, while signing the treaty, Collins said that he was signing his own 'death warrant'.

The Anglo–Irish Treaty of December 1921 marked a major advance on the Government of Ireland Act (1920), but it fell short of what Paul Bew, in *Ireland: The Politics of Enmity 1789–2006*, terms the 'very high level of expectancy' among nationalists. Most nationalists realised that some compromise was unavoidable, but a civil war ensued because of what Harry Boland saw at the time, and modern historians such as Michael Laffan, in *The Resurrection of Ireland*, see, as divisions between 'pragmatism and principle'.

The treaty offered Ireland the same dominion status as Canada, obliged Irish MPs to swear an oath of allegiance to a constitution in which the Crown was sovereign, allowed Britain to retain three 'treaty ports' and allowed Northern Ireland to opt out of the Irish Free State. Collins declared in the Dáil that the treaty gave Ireland 'freedom, not the ultimate freedom...but the freedom to achieve it'. Collins, Griffith and other pro-treaty members of Sinn Féin emphasised the tangible freedom secured through the treaty and argued that no better deal was possible at that time.

De Valera disagreed. Yet his alternative proposal, Document No. 2, was almost identical to the treaty, and simply copied its terms about Northern Ireland and the Boundary Commission, the treaty ports and finance. Collins dismissed it as 'splitting hairs', and Griffith said it was only a 'quibble' about words. De Valera's Document No. 2 omitted the oath and proposed 'external association' between Ireland and the commonwealth. It was a matter of symbolism — but, as Richard English acknowledges in *Irish Freedom*, symbols were extremely important to nationalists, and no less so to the British government. Belfast-born Seán MacEntee was the only TD (member of the Dáil) who spoke out about partition.

Reactions to the treaty were not just decided by pragmatism or principle. In the Dáil cabinet Brugha and Stack sided with de Valera against Collins and Griffith in opposition to the treaty, but relations between the two sides were very hostile before the truce. Many men decided for or against the treaty according to individual ties. The attitude of many men who supported the treaty was, 'If it's good enough for Mick [Collins], it's good enough for me.' However, Michael Laffan, in *The Resurrection of Ireland*, and Michael Hopkinson in *Green Against Green: The Irish Civil War*, find that several Sinn Féin TDs changed their minds in favour of the treaty after meeting constituents during the Christmas holidays. The Dáil cabinet split 4 to 3 in favour of the treaty. In the Dáil there were 64 votes in favour and 57 against. Yet in the country at large, public opinion was strongly in favour of the treaty. In the June 1922 general elections, pro-treaty Sinn Féin won 58 seats, as opposed to 36 anti-treaty TDs, while the other 34 TDs also supported the treaty. The great majority of public bodies in the Irish Free State, the county councils, chambers of commerce, trade unions and, crucially, the Catholic Church, also supported the treaty. However, as contemporaries noted, and modern historians such as Hopkinson confirm, there was no real enthusiasm for the treaty among nationalists. Most of them accepted it as the best that could be achieved at that time.

Civil war

Michael Hopkinson, the leading historian of the Irish civil war, shows in *Green Against Green* that most of the active IRA volunteers opposed the treaty. Richard Mulcahy, the IRA's chief of staff, called off an IRA convention in March 1922 because he knew that most would reject the treaty. Joe Lee, in *Ireland 1912–1985*, claims that the civil war was a contest between 'democracy and dictatorship', meaning that the anti-treaty IRA (or 'Irregulars' as they were called) were prepared to ignore the democratic wishes of the Irish people to dictate their own doctrinaire terms. Laffan and Fitzpatrick also highlight the anti-democratic mentality of anti-treaty IRA commanders such as Tom Barry, Liam Mellows and Rory O'Connor. Coogan is extremely critical of de Valera for fuelling anti-treaty feeling with bloodthirsty rhetoric. However, Richard English reminds us of the sincerity of the anti-treaty feeling that the republic, and the 'martyrs' who died for it, had been betrayed by a treaty that consented to Ireland's membership of the British empire.

Hopkinson highlights the reluctance with which the pro- and anti-treaty republicans went to war. There were 6 months during which earnest efforts were made to 'settle the political and military divisions', but they failed. The provisional government, headed by Michael Collins after the treaty was ratified by the Dáil, allowed local IRA commanders, regardless of their feelings towards the treaty, to take charge of barracks evacuated by the British Army. However, a clash between pro-treaty and anti-treaty IRA units about who should occupy a British barracks in Limerick in

March 1922 was followed by similar incidents that exposed the weakness of the provisional government's military position.

Collins, who was very concerned about the wellbeing of nationalists within the Northern Irish state, strongly encouraged IRA unity in a campaign in the province. From early 1922 there were IRA attacks on security positions north of the border, and guns were supplied to protect nationalists in Belfast from loyalist mobs. However, IRA attacks in border areas regularly provoked loyalist violence against Belfast's Catholic community. Attempts to reduce the bloodshed in Northern Ireland by means of the Craig–Collins pacts in January and March 1922 having failed, Collins and Liam Lynch, a leading opponent of the treaty, launched a joint IRA offensive against the unionist state in May and June 1922. However, the lack of local support, a lack of strategic planning and a lack of resources meant that it ended in failure.

The anti-treaty IRA set up an executive which, in Alvin Jackson's words, 'looked very like a military junta', to challenge the authority of Collins's provisional government. In April 1922 Rory O'Connor and other members of the anti-treaty executive occupied the Four Courts and other buildings in Dublin. The action was intended to symbolise their association with the rebels of 1916, and to provide an alternative focus for Irish loyalty. However, Collins insisted on taking no action against the Irregulars in Dublin, while the Irregulars themselves were careful not to start a war against the provisional government. In May 1922 Collins agreed to a pact with de Valera to avoid splitting Sinn Féin in two in the forthcoming general election. It involved agreeing to a panel of pro- and anti-treaty Sinn Féin candidates to be put to the electorate in proportion to their existing numbers in the Dáil. Hopkinson sees it as a desperate bid to prevent a civil war, but it failed.

Collins tried to frame the constitution of the Irish Free State in such a manner that it would be acceptable to both sides in Sinn Féin. However, Winston Churchill, as colonial secretary, with responsibility for Ireland as one of the dominions, insisted that the constitution be rewritten in May 1922 to conform to the 'dominion status' agreed in the Anglo–Irish Treaty. It was another aborted attempt to avoid a civil war.

By June 1922, after the IRA offensive along the border and the assassination in London of Sir Henry Wilson, the Northern Irish government's security adviser, Churchill was determined that the provisional Irish government should assert its authority, otherwise the British Army would take action against the Irregulars in Dublin. Under that direct threat Collins authorised the attack on the Irregulars in the Four Courts in Dublin on 27 June 1922. The civil war had begun.

Earlier in 1922 the provisional government had made a start in setting up a new National Army, formed around pro-treaty IRA men but including many new recruits, some of them former members of the British Army. It was short of experienced officers, but it soon became a professional army, by contrast with the Irregulars, who resorted to 'commandeering' private property to maintain themselves. People of property looked to the Irish Army for stability and order, while the Irregulars were disproportionately popular among the rural poor in western Ireland.

In terms of the fighting of the war, Alvin Jackson, in *Ireland*, reckons that 'perhaps the most crucial military resource that the Free State forces possessed was the support of the people'. He noted too that the blessing of the Catholic bishops in October 1922 was welcome. In addition, the National Army was well supplied with British Army guns and munitions. It had the financial resources of a state behind it, and plenty of recruits. By June 1923 the National Army had 50,000 soldiers. Collins and the National Army commanders showed more initiative and decisiveness than the Irregulars, who took up defensive positions from the start. Within 2 months the National Army had cleared the Irregulars from Dublin and from the rest of Ireland outside of the 'Cork republic'. On 8 August 1922, National Army soldiers landed behind the Irregulars' front lines from ships at Youghal, Cork harbour and Union Hall and quickly captured Cork city. The Irregulars then retreated into the hills of the southwest to fight a guerrilla war. Collins may have been attempting to talk peace with the Irregulars when he was ambushed and killed in west Cork in August 1922.

After Collins's death the Irish Free State government adopted increasingly stern measures to deal with the Irregulars. Roy Foster, in *Modern Ireland*, expresses the view that 'the Free State government had been confronted with a declared policy of shooting on sight elected TDs, legal officials, ex-British Army members and even sympathetic journalists: an extreme reaction was inevitable'. In September 1922 a Special Powers Act was passed by the Dáil. The Free State government sanctioned the execution of prisoners in reprisal for Irregulars' attacks, such as the assassination of Seán Hales, a pro-treaty TD. In all, 77 Irregulars were executed — a shocking action which demoralised the anti-treaty republicans. In addition there were unofficial killings of captured Irregulars by members of the National Army, most notoriously the Kerry killings of March 1923, at the 'fag end of the civil war'. Once the determined Irregular commander Liam Lynch was killed in April 1923 the violence petered out. Lynch's replacement, Frank Aiken, convinced the anti-treaty gunmen and their political allies to agree to a ceasefire. On 24 May 1923 the civil war was officially ended.

Hopkinson calculates that 800 soldiers in the National Army were killed in the civil war, and many more Irregulars. The death of Collins, in particular, was felt as a grievous loss at the time and for long afterwards. As Jackson declares, he was the 'best friend' of the northern nationalists in the Irish Free State government. The war cost the Free State government £17 million, and £30 million was paid in compensation to certain victims of the war, at a time when the government's annual budget was only £28 million. The civil war shattered illusions among nationalists, and left a legacy of bitterness in southern politics that persisted for decades. It also distracted southern attention away from Northern Ireland. Cahir Healy, a northern nationalist MP, was not alone in his community in feeling abandoned by the Irish government.

The Boundary Commission

The Free State government inherited Collins's and Griffith's assumption that the Boundary Commission to be established under Article 12 of the Anglo–Irish Treaty would resolve the issue of partition. The article directed that the border be redrawn 'in accordance with the wishes of the inhabitants'. Naively, perhaps, nationalists assumed that large areas in Northern Ireland with nationalist majorities, such as Fermanagh and Tyrone, Derry City and possibly south Armagh and south Down, would be transferred to the Free State. The very future of the 'rump' of Northern Ireland was seen to be in doubt. However, because of the civil war in the Free State and Ulster unionist hostility in the north, the Boundary Commission was not established until October 1924.

By then Cumann na nGaedheal, the Irish government party, was officially committed to a 'pacific and gradualist approach to reunification'. However, as Alvin Jackson astutely comments in *Ireland,* in practice, 'Free State policy towards Northern Ireland was a self-defeating mixture of consensual rhetoric, petty coercion and an increasingly passive sympathy with Ulster Catholics.' It served to antagonise northern unionists, but made life more difficult, not better, for northern nationalists. In April 1923 the Free State set up a chain of customs posts along the border, giving it, in Ronan Fanning's words, 'a permanence and physical appearance it had not had previously'.

The Free State government nominated Eóin Mac Néill, a prominent northern nationalist, to represent it on the Boundary Commission. Northern Ireland was represented by J. R. Fisher, while the three-man commission was chaired by Richard Feetham, a judge from South Africa. Feetham and Fisher combined to interpret the meaning of Article 12 in a resolutely conservative manner. They decided that only very small areas would be transferred. That alone would have shocked nationalists, given their unrealistic expectations. However, the commission proposed that parts of the Irish Free State, mostly in County Donegal, would be returned to the UK. When Fisher leaked the outlines of the Boundary Commission's report to the *Morning Post* it created a crisis for the Free State government. The thought of putting any part of the Free State back under British rule was against all shades of nationalist opinion, and it threatened to undermine the uneasy peace secured after the civil war.

At a hastily convened meeting of the London, Dublin and Belfast governments it was agreed to suppress the report of the Boundary Commission. To appease the Northern Irish government the Council of Ireland was scrapped. The Free State government's liability to pay a share of Britain's war debts was cancelled. It was a shameful end to the Free State's hopes of a united Ireland. It also provided an excuse for Éamon de Valera to overcome his scruples about taking the oath to enter the Dáil as leader of Fianna Fáil. Some northern nationalist MPs decided to end their boycott of the Belfast parliament in 1925 in the vain hope of achieving some kind of accommodation for their community with the Northern Irish state.

What problems confronted the Northern Ireland government in the period 1920–25?

Russell Rees, in *Ireland 1900–25*, observes that the Ulster unionists had achieved 'a major success' in the establishment of Northern Ireland. However, the new state faced a number of problems, not least the hostility of a large minority of its citizens. The Northern Irish state succeeded, through diplomacy with London and brute force at home, in consolidating its power. The shelving of the Boundary Commission in 1925 ended potential threats to its immediate future but, to quote the title of one of Patrick Buckland's books, it proved to be a 'factory of grievances' from the start, and deep instability persisted under the surface.

It has already been remarked that Sir James Craig used his influence in the coalition government to shape the Government of Ireland Act (1920) to his liking. Graham Walker, in *A History of the Ulster Unionist Party*, shows how hard Craig worked to see the act implemented. Roy Foster, in *Modern Ireland*, notes that administrative partition was already a fact even before the Act was passed. Twenty administrative experts were sent to Northern Ireland from Westminster to set up the new administrative structures for the province. Three hundred civil servants volunteered to be transferred from Dublin to Belfast, bringing valuable experience to the new civil service.

It was not until 3 May 1921 that the Government of Ireland Act officially came into effect, with elections in Northern Ireland 3 weeks later. Unionists won 40 of the 52 seats in the Belfast parliament, with six each going to Sinn Féin and the Nationalist Party (formerly the IPP). Craig moved quickly to form a Northern Irish cabinet and government. All historians of the period, including Walker, Rees and Jackson, are agreed that Craig was anxious to consolidate the Northern state as soon as possible because he did not trust British politicians not to make concessions to appease Sinn Féin.

To deal with nationalists' non-cooperation in Fermanagh, Tyrone and Derry city the unionist government suspended the local councils. New local elections were organised without proportional representation and with gerrymandered constituencies to give the unionists control of all local governments in Northern Ireland. Collins complained strongly to London about such undemocratic measures, but Rees points out that British objections were silenced by Craig's threat to resign. Walker criticises nationalists for not participating in the process for drawing up constituency boundaries, but it is certain that they would not have been listened to in any case. In the event, Walker states that the unionist councils were able to pursue their 'sectarian agendas' and their wish to 'keep down rates' at the expense of poor Catholics. He observes that London turned a blind eye to 'partisan' and 'corrupt' practices in Northern Ireland, as British politicians were more than keen to disengage from Irish affairs.

As English and Hart have shown in their studies of the IRA, Northern Ireland escaped much of the violence of the Anglo–Irish War, which was concentrated in southwestern Ireland and Dublin. However, in June 1920 there was a clash between the IRA and the RIC in Derry. Former members of the Ulster Volunteer Force remobilised against an exaggerated nationalist/republican threat. Tensions ran extremely high during the 'marching season' of that year. On 17 July 1920 an RIC officer from Ulster was killed by the IRA in Cork. Loyalists then forced thousands of Catholic workers from their jobs in the Belfast shipyards and engineering factories and attacked Catholic homes. When Inspector Swanzy from Lisburn was killed by the IRA in Cork, in retaliation for the murder of the Sinn Féin Lord Mayor of Cork, Tomás MacCurtain, loyalists launched violent attacks against Catholics in Lisburn, Belfast and elsewhere, forcing many to flee from their homes. Hart points out that 8,000 Catholics were driven from their homes, 6,000 were expelled from their jobs, and 'well over' 300 were killed and almost 1,000 wounded by loyalists. The 'Belfast boycott' organised in retaliation by Sinn Féin did nothing to improve the situation.

Loyalist paramilitaries and vigilantes threatened to undermine the Ulster unionists' position in the eyes of the British public through such violent sectarianism. To deal with the republican threat, and to bring the loyalist vigilantes under some kind of control, Craig persuaded the British government to establish the Ulster Special Constabulary (USC) in October 1920, though Rees writes that there were doubts in London about the wisdom of arming loyalists. Nonetheless, soon there were 3,500 full-time USC officers, and 16,000 B Specials, in addition to the RIC. According to Rees, the bulk of the USC were former members of the UVF.

The violence in Northern Ireland was concentrated in Belfast, where loyalist mobs attacked Catholics in what has been called a 'pogrom'. The police were involved in some of the murders, including the infamous murder of the McMahon family. However, both English and Hart point out that after the initial attacks, some Catholics in Belfast secured guns to defend their community against the loyalists, and a cycle of tit-for-tat violence broke out in 1921 and 1922, with Protestants suffering a third of casualties and the Catholic minority two-thirds. Craig visited de Valera on 5 May 1921 to discuss ways of reducing communal violence, and he met Collins twice in 1922, but nothing was achieved.

Following the truce in summer 1921 there was a lull in the violence. However, communal violence gradually resumed. On 7 April 1922 the Northern Irish government introduced the Special Powers Act for 1 year — though it was renewed year after year until it became permanent. Rees points out that while London objected to the Belfast government taking such draconian powers, it did not veto the Act because it was glad that the Northern Irish government was relieving it of responsibility for

Ulster's problems. On 22 May 1922 a unionist MP was murdered, and internment was introduced. The vast majority of the internees were Catholics. Collins stepped up the IRA attacks on border areas, and occupied part of Fermanagh for a time, but the British Army intervened in support of the newly established Royal Ulster Constabulary (RUC) and the USC.

Once the civil war got underway in the Irish Free State, IRA pressure on Northern Ireland was greatly reduced, and it ended almost completely when Collins was killed in August 1922. In all, 428 people were killed in the 'Troubles' in the North. Northern Ireland's security was assured, but the violence, and the incorporation of loyalist paramilitaries, including the murderous Ulster Protestant Association, into the USC, caused deep resentment.

Walker shows that the Ulster unionists were very anxious about the Boundary Commission that was authorised by the Anglo–Irish Treaty of 1921. Collins and the Sinn Féin delegates were led to believe by Lloyd George that substantial nationalist areas would be transferred to the Irish Free State, though Lloyd George reassured Conservatives and unionists that only minor changes to the border were envisaged. In the event, the civil war in the South delayed the establishment of the Boundary Commission until 1924, and its report, recommending very minor changes, was suppressed at the Irish government's request. The border was left unchanged and the Council of Ireland was abolished. Walker says the episode ended 'satisfactorily' from the unionists' point of view, but it also showed that the close relationship between the Conservatives and the Ulster unionists had ended. Walker emphasises that successive British governments were happy to ignore Northern Irish affairs, while Craig and the Ulster unionists were no less keen to avoid 'interference' from London.

One area that continued to involve London was finance. Northern Ireland's economy, heavily dependent on old-style shipbuilding, engineering and textile industries, experienced a severe downturn in the postwar slump. The Belfast government tried to prop up these old industries but failed to attract new ones. Both Catholics and Protestants suffered from increased unemployment, but Catholics suffered most because of being expelled from their jobs and because of discrimination. Buckland shows how the economic downturn threatened to bankrupt the Northern Irish government until the Colwyn Committee in 1925 reduced the 'imperial contribution' payable by Northern Ireland and subsidised social welfare payments. Nonetheless, the failure of Craig's government to address the fundamental underlying problems in the Northern Irish economy ensured that poverty was widespread and persistent in the new state.

Walker shows how Craig's initial efforts to encourage Catholics to join the RUC, and to promote a couple of Catholics to his government, were soon abandoned. The first minister for education, Lord Londonderry, made efforts to create an integrated education system in Northern Ireland. However, Londonderry appointed a vocal critic of the Catholic Church, Robert Lynn, to head the committee to design the new education system. His recommendations were opposed by the Catholic

Church because it was keen to preserve its own schools system and all nationalists were deeply distrustful of the unionist government. The abstention of the Catholic schools made it easier for the Protestant churches to cooperate with Londonderry. In the Education Act (1923) a non-denominational education system was set up with full state funding, while Catholic schools outside the system were given reduced funding. Under pressure from the Protestant churches and the Orange Order, Bible instruction was provided in the supposedly non-denominational state schools from 1925, and Protestant clergymen were given more say in the appointment of teachers. Londonderry's scheme for integrated education had the unintended result that Catholic children were educated in schools that were less well funded than those attended by Protestant children. He resigned as education minister in January 1926.

David Harkness, in *Northern Ireland Since 1920*, is only one of the historians who emphasise the Ulster unionists' genuine fears for their security that fuelled their 'siege mentality'. Craig succeeded, however, in establishing a functioning Northern Irish state that was secure from the large minority of people inside its borders who were hostile to it, and from the threat from the IRA in border areas. By the end of 1925 the future of Northern Ireland was secure, and Craig was later to boast that unionists had 'a Protestant state for a Protestant people'. However, the bloody birth of Northern Ireland and what Laffan terms the 'petty sectarianism' of its rulers sowed seeds for future trouble.

Glossary

Act of Union The Act of Parliament that created the United Kingdom of Great Britain and Ireland in 1801. Those who support the Union are known as unionists.

Dáil Éireann The Irish parliament established by Sinn Féin in January 1919.

Dominion The dominions, Canada, Australia, New Zealand and South Africa, were territories which enjoyed self-government but were part of the British empire.

Home Rule A form of devolved government which would have established an Irish government with jurisdiction over a restricted range of domestic matters, while Ireland remained part of the United Kingdom and subject to the Crown and the UK Parliament at Westminster.

Irish Citizen Army (ICA) This was established in 1913 to provide protection for striking workers in Dublin. Its leader, James Connolly, decided to use the ICA to launch a Socialist revolution in Ireland during the course of the Great War.

Irish Republican Army (IRA) In 1919 the Irish Volunteers were formally recognised as the army of the Irish republic by the first Dáil. The Irish Volunteers were originally established in 1913 in response to the establishment of the Ulster Volunteer Force. Its leadership was infiltrated by IRB activists who hoped to deploy the movement for republican goals.

Irish Republican Brotherhood (IRB)   The IRB was a conspiratorial organisation that aspired to make Ireland an independent republic. Its members were known as 'Fenians', a synonym for 'republican'. The IRB concentrated its efforts on promoting separatist sentiment by infiltrating 'new nationalism' movements such as the GAA and the Gaelic League, and later the Irish Volunteers.

Teachta Dála (TD)   A member of the Irish parliament from 1919.

Ulster Special Constabulary (USC)   This paramilitary police force was established in 1920 to contain the threat posed by the IRA in Ulster. Its members included former members of the UVF and loyalist vigilantes.

Key figures

Herbert Asquith   Leader of the Liberal Party and prime minister of the UK, 1908–16. He proved to be a weak leader at times of stress, as shown during the Home Rule crisis and during the Great War.

Edward Carson   A Protestant from Dublin. Leader of the Ulster Unionist Party and the Irish Unionist Alliance from 1910 to 1921. His initial intention was to use the Ulster unionists to prevent any part of Ireland from securing Home Rule. However, by late 1913 he came to realise that while the Ulster unionists enjoyed considerable public support in Great Britain, there was a general feeling that most of Ireland should be given Home Rule. Carson was the key strategist in the Ulster unionists' campaign against Home Rule, their most effective orator and their main link with the Conservative establishment in England. He enjoyed brief spells as a member of the British coalition government from May 1915. He resigned as leader of the Ulster unionists in February 1921 in favour of his deputy, James Craig, because he felt that, as a southern unionist, he might not be effective as the prime minister of Northern Ireland.

Winston Churchill   He was promoted to Prime Minister Asquith's cabinet in 1908. He was Home Secretary from 1910 to 1911, and First Lord of the Admiralty until 1915. He was one of the most talented members of the government, and his views on Irish affairs carried weight. He was one of the earliest ministers to recommend exclusion of part of Ulster to defuse the Home Rule crisis. As Secretary of State for War from January 1919 and as Secretary of State for the Colonies from 1920 he was deeply involved in Irish affairs and was a signatory to the Anglo–Irish Treaty (1921).

Tom Clarke   A veteran Fenian who returned to Ireland some years after serving a prison sentence for his part in an Irish Republican Brotherhood campaign in Britain. Arguably he was the mastermind of the 1916 Rising, though he set up Patrick Pearse as the figurehead of the rising to widen its appeal to young nationalists. He was executed soon after the rising had ended.

James Connolly   Born to Irish parents in Scotland, Connolly was a Marxist with an international reputation before the Great War. In 1913 he established the Irish Citizen Army (ICA) to protect striking workers in Dublin. Once the war broke out he decided to use the ICA to spearhead a Socialist revolution in Ireland. Connolly played a key role in the 1916 Rising. He was executed soon after the rising ended.

James Craig   Unionist MP for East Down, 1906–18, and for Mid-Down, 1918–21. He was staunchly Protestant and a member of the Orange Order. Craig was an indifferent orator, but his organisational skills were impressive. He made a very effective deputy to Edward Carson, whom he succeeded as leader of the Ulster unionists in February 1921. Craig became Northern Ireland's first prime minister in June 1921.

Joseph Devlin   Irish Parliamentary Party MP for West Belfast from 1906. He was a self-made man with a fierce commitment to improving the lot of the Catholic community in Ulster. He was Grand Master of the Ancient Order of Hibernians, a Catholic counterpart to the Orange Order. He was recognised as the leading northern nationalist. However, he misled his southern colleagues as to the threat posed by the UVF for fear of partition. He served as a nationalist MP until his death in 1934.

John Dillon   Deputy leader of the IPP from 1900 to 1918, when he succeeded John Redmond as leader. Dillon was more radical than Redmond. While he was always loyal to his leader, it was noticeable that he did not join Redmond in encouraging Irish men to join the British Army in the Great War. He was in Dublin during the 1916 Rising and witnessed the radicalisation of Irish nationalists in its aftermath. He tried to inject new energy into the IPP on becoming its leader in March 1918, but it was too late. Dillon lost his seat in the general election of December 1918.

David Lloyd George   Chancellor of the Exchequer in Asquith's government from 1908 to 1915, and prime minister from 1916 to 1922, Lloyd George was a man of exceptional energy and talent. He played an increasingly important role in Irish affairs, as for example in the 1916 talks he held with Carson and Redmond. When he was prime minister his policy towards Ireland reflected British concerns for the integrity of the UK and the British empire. Only when public opinion baulked at the political and military costs of escalating the Anglo–Irish War in Ireland in June 1921 did Lloyd George set about devising and securing a settlement for Ireland that would satisfy most people in Britain and Ireland. He lost his place as prime minister in 1922 following revelations of corrupt practices.

Patrick Pearse   A romantic nationalist who founded an Irish language school, edited the Gaelic League's newspaper and was a leading member of the Irish Volunteers. He was recruited into the IRB by Tom Clarke. Clarke recognised that Pearse's youth, idealism and eloquence would make him useful as the figurehead for the 1916 Rising. He was executed soon after the rising had ended.

John Redmond   Leader of the IPP from 1900 to 1918. He was a genial politician who earnestly argued that Irish nationalists should embrace Ireland's membership of the UK once Ireland had been granted Home Rule. However, Redmond failed to address effectively the challenge posed by the Ulster unionists, and lost the initiative to them. From 1914 Redmond found himself responding helplessly to events, and he had lost the confidence of most of the nationalist electorate before he died in March 1918.

Éamon de Valera   The American-born son of a Spaniard and an Irishwoman, he grew up in Ireland after his father's death. He was the most senior Irish Volunteer commander not to have been executed after the 1916 Rising, because of his American citizenship. In 1917 he was elected as MP for East Clare and became the president of Sinn Féin. He brought together the militant and constitutional strands of the republican movement.

Questions
&
Answers

This part of the Student Unit Guide contains advice on how to answer examination questions on 'Partition of Ireland 1900–25', and offers specimen questions and answers. Half of the marks for this unit are awarded for questions relating to three sources (though answers to the source questions must include the use of your own knowledge), and half of the marks are awarded for an essay. In terms of timing, you are advised to spend more time on the source questions than on the essay, because the sources will require careful reading and consideration before you attempt to answer the questions posed.

The questions in this section have been adapted from CCEA examination questions. The specimen answers provided are not authentic answers produced by CCEA candidates under examination conditions.

Section A: Source evaluation and analysis

Read the sources and answer the questions which follow.

Source 1

Extract from a speech by the Prime Minister, David Lloyd George, to the House of Commons, 10 December 1920. He was commenting on government policy during the Anglo–Irish War of 1919–21.

> The government has been in touch with intermediaries in order to end this bloody conflict. While the majority of the people of Ireland are anxious for a peaceful settlement, the government is convinced that the Sinn Féin Party, which controls those responsible for murder and outrage, is not yet ready for a peaceful settlement based on the maintenance of unity with the United Kingdom. Therefore I declare the dual policy of the government. First, we will continue to open every channel to help bring about an honourable settlement. Secondly, we will take all necessary steps to crush those who are using murder and outrage against the forces of the Crown. We will introduce martial law in the southwest of Ireland and treat the rebels in the same way as they treat the forces of the Crown. Those who illegally carry arms will be treated as rebels and will be sentenced to death by a military court. The same penalty will be applied to those who give assistance to such rebels.

Source 2

Extract from a declaration issued by seven Church of England bishops and 13 leaders of the Protestant churches in Great Britain, 5 April 1921. They were commenting on the policy of reprisals used by the Crown's forces during the Anglo–Irish War.

> We fully support the recent statement by the Archbishop of Canterbury, who has condemned the deplorable practice of reprisals by the forces of the Crown. We believe that the cruel outrages committed by republicans are due more to political grievances, caused by government policy, than criminal intent. We plead with the government to arrange a genuine truce and settle the Irish difficulty. The policy of reprisals is causing grave unrest throughout the [British] empire, arouses hostile criticism from other friendly nations and deepens the feeling of alienation between this country and the Irish people. A method of government which uses reprisals cannot be politically or morally right.

Source 3

Extract from Paul Canning, *British Policy Towards Ireland, 1921–1941*, published in 1985. Canning is commenting on the truce that ended the Anglo–Irish War in July 1921:

> The truce came at a convenient time for both sides. In May 1921 the government believed that a successful summer offensive would require 100,000 troops, more reprisals and a widening of martial law. The prospect of a winter campaign was equally unattractive to the forces of the crown. The policy of reprisals was causing a storm of protest in England. As for the IRA, the truce came at a time when it was beginning to run short of arms and ammunition, while manpower shortages were caused by arrests based on improved British intelligence.

By permission of Oxford University Press.

Part (a)

Consult all of the sources and your knowledge of this period. Which of the sources would an historian value most in a study of the Anglo–Irish War of 1919–21?   **(15 marks)**

■ ■ ■

High A-grade answer

A historian would value all three sources in a study of the Anglo–Irish War. However, I will argue that Source 1 is the most valuable of the three.

> ✒ **The introduction addresses the question of 'value' directly. It identifies the source which a historian would value most. It is important to identify one source as the most valuable, otherwise your argument will seem confused or confusing. Do not worry if you have difficulty identifying which particular source is of most 'value'. The examiner looks at the persuasiveness of your argument; what reasons you offer to support your choice of the most valuable source, and what evidence you cite to support your argument.**

Source 3 is valuable because it gives a professional historian's explanation of how the war came to an end. A good historian would study all of the primary sources available, analyse them professionally and form objective and well-argued conclusions. Source 3 is most valuable in showing the reader how both sides in the Anglo–Irish War were willing to agree to a truce by July 1921. It points to the military demands of the war — 100,000 more soldiers were required according to General Macready, the commander-in-chief of the British Army in Ireland. Also, Macready demanded the right to extend martial law across more of Ireland, and to step up the campaign of reprisals. Yet Peter Hart, in his book *The IRA at War*, has shown how support for the IRA grew in response to violent actions by the British Army, the RIC, the 'Black and Tans' and the Auxiliaries. Also, the reprisals caused 'a storm of protest in England'. On the other hand, Source 3 is of value too in pointing to the problems facing the IRA by the summer of 1921; the 'manpower shortages' caused by the increasing numbers of arrests of republicans, and the shortage of 'arms and ammunition'. The fact that both sides were under pressure by the summer of 1921 helps to explain why they both agreed to a truce.

This short extract does not address other key factors which led the British government to decide on a truce. For example, Alan O'Day, in *Irish Home Rule*, argues that the fact that a Northern Irish government had been elected in June 1921 was crucial. Therefore, I do not think that Source 3 would be of most value to a historian studying the Anglo–Irish War.

> ✒ **The value of the source for studying the Anglo–Irish War is assessed by using a range of criteria: its date, author, motive and mode, and the information it communicates. All of the information provided about**

the source has been used to assess its value. The question required the deployment of the student's 'own knowledge', which is duly provided. The answer recognises that although the source is secondary, it still has value to a historian. It explains in some detail why it is valuable, and indicates what is most valuable about it. It also outlines some limitations of the source. A good historian will read what other historians have written on a subject, but the most valuable sources for any historian are primary sources. The discussion of the source is concluded with a summary statement about its value to a historian studying the Anglo–Irish War.

Source 2 is a valuable source because it quotes part of a public declaration made by 20 leaders of the Protestant churches in Great Britain in response to British government policy during the Anglo–Irish War, and it may have influenced the subsequent direction of that policy. It is a very valuable source for indicating public attitudes to the government's policy towards Ireland, and for showing some of the pressure Lloyd George's government was under to change its policy.

Source 2 is of value for highlighting the key aspect of the government's policy which was criticised, 'the deplorable practice of reprisals', which they stated was not 'politically or morally right'. They stated that the reprisals were causing 'grave unrest throughout the empire' and arousing 'hostile criticism from other friendly nations'. Their statement points to the international effects of the reprisals policy in Ireland. The churchmen indicated also that the policy of reprisals was counter-productive and deepened the 'feeling of alienation' between the Irish people and Britain. They criticised the 'cruel outrages committed by republicans', but they urged the government to arrange a 'genuine truce' and 'settle the Irish difficulty'. The churchmen's declaration supported the Archbishop of Canterbury's condemnation of the policy of reprisals.

However, it cannot be shown that the churchmen's declaration of 5 April 1921 affected the British government's decision to call a truce 3 months later. It is of value in highlighting the kind of pressure the government was coming under. Yet, by itself, this source may give a misleading impression of the influence that the churchmen exerted on government policy.

Again, the value of the source is evaluated against a range of criteria. Why it is valuable is clearly stated. No less importantly, its limitations are highlighted. The answer is based on a thorough analysis of the source itself, and also on the student's 'own knowledge', which puts the source in context and helps to assess its value to a historian studying the Anglo–Irish War.

I think that Source 1 would be of most value to a historian studying the Anglo–Irish War. It is an extract from a speech made by Prime Minister Lloyd George, arguably the most important individual in the Anglo–Irish War. He was in charge of the British government's political and military policies towards Ireland. The timing of the speech is significant in that it followed on from the controversy surrounding the reprisals at

Balbriggan, the massacre at Croke Park and the burning of Cork city centre. Lloyd George signalled his commitment to that policy, and to extending it.

The speech is of great value to a historian in showing that Lloyd George's government was in contact with 'intermediaries' and was prepared to consider an 'honourable settlement' — but in December 1920 that still meant maintaining 'unity with the United Kingdom'. Lloyd George believed that an increased military campaign against the republicans would make Sinn Féin 'ready' for such a settlement in time. Hence, Lloyd George emphasised that his government would take 'all necessary steps to crush' the IRA. That meant introducing martial law in the southwest, where the IRA was most active, and using military courts to sentence to death not only people who 'illegally' carried arms but also anyone who gave 'assistance to such rebels'.

The tone of Lloyd George's speech is one of determination. It lends support to O'Leary and Maume, who argue that the decision of the British government to propose a truce in July 1921 was taken very shortly beforehand, after the establishment of Northern Ireland in June 1921 simplified the 'Irish Question' from a British point of view, and after Macready's pessimistic assessment of the military situation. I think that a historian would find Source 1 the most valuable for a study of the Anglo–Irish War.

In terms of its limitations, one has to remember that speeches are normally made to persuade an audience. That means that a historian cannot be entirely confident that a speech will provide an entirely full, accurate or true account of its subject matter. Lloyd George was unlikely to express any doubts about his policy's prospects for success, or accept any responsibility for the terrible situation in Ireland. A historian would need to look for other sources, such as diaries or confidential papers, to see if the public statements of the prime minister were consistent with what he wrote or said privately, or among people he trusted. Nonetheless, this source remains of most value to a historian studying the Anglo–Irish War because it shows what Lloyd George wanted the British Parliament and people to believe at the time that he made the speech. It may also show what he actually believed at a critical time during the war.

> **Discussing the most valuable source last helped to emphasise its value, and facilitated a clear presentation of the argument. The answer repeatedly emphasises the value of the source to a historian studying the Anglo–Irish War. It uses the student's 'own knowledge' as well as the source itself to assess its value. It identifies limitations in the source.**

■ ■ ■

Part (b)

Use all the sources and other evidence you have studied. How far do the sources support the view that the truce of July 1921 was an unexpected conclusion to the Anglo–Irish War? (20 marks)

■ ■ ■

High A-grade answer

Source 1, an extract from a speech delivered by Prime Minister Lloyd George in the House of Commons on 10 December 1920, would certainly not lead one to expect that the Anglo–Irish War would end in a truce in July 1921. Lloyd George said he was determined not to give way to 'murder and outrage'. He was determined to deal with the republican 'murder gangs' by escalating British military actions. He talked about taking 'all necessary steps' to 'crush' the IRA. He talked about introducing martial law in the southwest of Ireland, and about using military courts to impose death sentences not only on 'rebels' who carried arms illegally but also on 'those who give assistance to such rebels'. Lloyd George's warning that the Crown's forces would 'treat the rebels in the same way as they treat the forces of the Crown' gave public sanction to the policy of reprisals, and even encouraged it.

Nonetheless, Lloyd George's speech hinted at his government being open to the possibility of negotiations with Sinn Féin. The speech indicates that the government had been 'in touch with intermediaries to end this bloody conflict'. That suggests that a truce at some point in the future was not entirely 'unexpected'. However, a truce 7 months later could not have been expected.

Nicholas Mansergh, in *The Unresolved Question*, shows that as late as June 1921 the British government was still committed to destroying republicanism by military means. When Sinn Féin boycotted the parliament established for Southern Ireland by the Government of Ireland Act (1920), the British government decided on 2 June 1921 to extend martial law across all of Southern Ireland. Neville Macready, the head of the British Army in Ireland, was asked to make the necessary preparations.

> ✎ **The discussion of Source 1 is clearly focused on the question about whether the truce was an unexpected conclusion to the Anglo–Irish War. It relates what Lloyd George stated in the House of Commons to the truce in the following year. It indicates how the source suggests that the truce of June 1921 was 'unexpected' at the time of the prime minister's speech in the House of Commons, but it highlights subtle nuances in the speech that allowed for the possibility of talks with Sinn Féin at some point in the future. Extensive use is made of 'other evidence' provided by the student, both factual and historiographical. Half of the marks for this question are awarded for 'other evidence'.**

Source 2, an extract from a public declaration made by 20 Protestant church leaders in Great Britain in April 1921, makes a truce that summer seem less 'unexpected'. The declaration was made in support of an earlier statement by the Archbishop of Canterbury that criticised the 'deplorable practice of reprisals by the forces of the Crown'. The church leaders condemned it 'politically' and 'morally'. Russell Rees, in *Ireland*, points out that 'the sheer brutality of "Bloody Sunday" shocked opinion in Ireland and Britain'. Diarmaid Ferriter, in *The Transformation of Ireland*, highlights Sinn Féin's success in publicising the 'reprisals' through the *Irish Bulletin*. The *Manchester Guardian* also did much to arouse British public opinion against the reprisals.

The church leaders referred to the 'grave unrest throughout the empire' caused by the British government's policy in Ireland. For Mansergh, that was a key problem for the British government. Mansergh, and Francis Costello, in *The Irish Revolution*, highlight the importance of Smuts in causing a change in government policy towards Ireland. The churchmen's reference to the 'hostile criticism' from 'other friendly nations' pinpointed another key consideration Lloyd George could not ignore. In particular, the British government was concerned about US opinion. This source suggests that by April 1921 a truce was no longer an 'unexpected conclusion' to the Anglo–Irish War, but Lloyd George and his government were not prepared to contemplate a truce until early in June 1921.

> **The discussion of Source 2 is sharply focused on the question posed, about whether the truce was an 'unexpected conclusion to the Anglo–Irish War'. There is thorough analysis of the source, informed by 'other evidence'. It highlights the growing pressure on the British government to call for a truce, but provides 'other evidence' to show that the government was very reluctant to bow to public pressure.**

Source 3, which quotes a modern historian's comments on the circumstances surrounding the truce, states that a successful military policy in Ireland would have required 100,000 troops, more reprisals and a widening of martial law at a time when the policy of reprisals was 'causing a storm of protest in England'. Even then Macready, the head of the British Army in Ireland, was very pessimistic about the prospects for success. He warned that 250,000 soldiers might be needed for success. Macready also demanded the right to execute Sinn Féin leaders at will, including de Valera and Griffith. His attitude was 'all out, or get out'. Nicholas Mansergh, in *The Unresolved Question*, writes that such draconian measures shocked the cabinet, and persuaded it to agree on the need for some kind of compromise with Sinn Féin. A truce might have been 'unexpected' at the end of 1920, but there was a lot of pressure on Lloyd George's government to concede a truce 6 months later.

Source 3 also points to the pressure on the IRA to agree to a truce. All historians agree that the Anglo–Irish War had reached a stalemate by July 1921. Diarmaid Ferriter agrees that the IRA was close to achieving a military stalemate and won a propaganda victory against the British by the summer of 1921. Charles Townshend's verdict is that the IRA's achievement was to 'ensure its survival for long enough to achieve psychological victory out of military stalemate'. Richard English, in *Irish Freedom*, concludes that 'the IRA could not simply be defeated'.

On the other hand, in 1921 the IRA suffered major setbacks. In March 1921 its GHQ in Dublin was raided by the British Army. The IRA suffered heavy losses in the Customs House in May 1921. In fact, by then 5,500 IRA volunteers were imprisoned. In addition, there was a crippling lack of weapons: Richard English quotes an IRA commander from County Longford stating that the IRA had guns for only a fraction of the men available. Michael Collins told the chief secretary for Ireland, Hamar Greenwood, 'We could not have lasted another three weeks.' As Source 3 states, 'Both sides were willing to consider the possibility of ending the violence and discussing a compromise settlement.'

Source 1 certainly gives the impression that the truce of July 1921 was 'unexpected', but Source 2 indicates that the British government was under growing political pressure to reconsider its policy towards Ireland. Source 3 adds a military dimension in its discussion of why the British government decided to call a truce in July 1921. Source 3 also helps to explain why the IRA was willing to agree to a truce. However, the three sources do not provide a full explanation of why the truce was called. As Alvin Jackson, in *Ireland*, remarks, 'It was not just that the IRA was shooting its way into the purview of the British cabinet.'

According to Alan O'Day in *Irish Home Rule*, the establishment of Northern Ireland left the British government free to address Sinn Féin in Southern Ireland. Smuts, the South African leader, played a key role in persuading the British government to use the opportunity provided by King George V's speech for the opening of the Belfast parliament to signal an openness to negotiate with Sinn Féin. Mansergh and Costello agree that the positive response to the king's speech persuaded Lloyd George to try for a settlement. The offer of dominion status for 26 counties, with security guarantees for the UK, and an acceptance of Northern Ireland's existence was agreed by Lloyd Gorge's cabinet before the truce was announced.

The answer uses a great deal of 'other evidence', especially the views of historians, to address the question of whether the truce of June 1921 was an 'unexpected conclusion' to the Anglo–Irish War. It argues that there were convincing reasons for both sides to agree to the calling of the truce by June 1921, though those reasons are not fully reflected in the three sources provided in the examination paper.

■ ■ ■

Section B: Historical interpretations

Question 1

'Although John Redmond seemed to have most reason to be satisfied with the outcome of the Third Home Rule crisis by September 1914, the real winners were Edward Carson and James Craig.' How far do you agree with this view? Use relevant evidence you have studied, including contemporary and later interpretations, to support your answer. (35 marks)

■■■

High A-grade answer

When on 18 September 1914 the Third Home Rule Bill was enacted, Redmond and the IPP seemed to be the 'winners' in the Third Home Rule Bill crisis. Carson and Craig, like unionists generally, were very upset at its enactment and walked out of the House of Commons in protest. They seemed to be the losers. However, with the advantage of hindsight, I believe that Carson and Craig, and the Ulster unionists in what would become Northern Ireland in 1920, were actually the real 'winners'. Yet Carson, a southern unionist, was not as much a 'winner' as Craig.

> 📝 The introduction addresses the question directly. It identifies the key players in the Home Rule crisis, and indicates what the argument outlined in the essay will be. It highlights the contrast between appearance and reality, and makes the important point that Carson, as a southern unionist, had a different agenda to the Ulster unionists whom he led.

Redmond became the leader of a united IPP on 6 February 1900. As an imperialist, he hoped that Ireland would play a significant role within the British empire once it had been granted Home Rule, a form of devolved government. His party had campaigned in vain for decades. Most historians, including Roy Foster in *Modern Ireland*, think that Redmond was powerless to influence his Liberal allies. However, O'Leary and Maume, in *Controversial Issues*, credit Redmond with a significant success in using the balance of power in the Commons to persuade Prime Minister Asquith to resolve the constitutional crisis surrounding the People's Budget by abolishing the Lords' veto in the Parliament Act of 1911. Nicholas Mansergh, in *The Unresolved Question*, states that Redmond had 'almost every cause for satisfaction' at that point because the Lords' veto seemed to be the last obstacle to Ireland's securing Home Rule. With the submission of the Third Home Rule Bill to the House of Commons in April 1912, Redmond and the IPP were confident that Home Rule was inevitable. O'Leary and Maume find that in their correspondence the nationalist politicians thought that it was 'in the bag'.

The context of the Home Rule crisis shows how nationalists were confident of being the 'winners' before events unfolded in 1912–14. Considerable weight is given to the interpretations of historians, which is required if the student is to secure a top grade.

If nationalists were confident about being the 'winners', the prospects for the unionists looked bleak. Yet by promoting Edward Carson MP, a Dublin barrister, as their leader, the Ulster unionists transformed their position. Carson visited Ulster for only the second time in his life in September 1911 to see for himself the strength of Ulster unionists' determination to fight Home Rule. He told James Craig, the leading Ulster unionist, that he was 'not for a mere game of bluff'. Craig organised a demonstration of 50,000 Orangemen and other unionists in the grounds of his house at Craigavon and won Carson to their cause. Yet Carson was a southern unionist. He planned to harness Ulster unionist opposition to prevent any part of Ireland securing Home Rule. He told a meeting of southern unionists in Dublin on 10 October 1911, 'If Ulster succeeds, Home Rule is dead.'

Carson and Craig spearheaded a very successful campaign to highlight Ulster Protestants' opposition to Home Rule. Carson's oratory and connections with the Conservative establishment in Great Britain, and Craig's organisational skills and contacts on the ground, made them a formidable team. They were joined in the fight against Home Rule by the new leader of the Conservative Party, Andrew Bonar Law, whose family came from Coleraine in Ulster. Mansergh sees Bonar Law's becoming the Conservative leader as crucial to the outcome of the Home Rule crisis. No other Conservative would have backed Carson and Craig as fiercely as Bonar Law did.

Bonar Law's speech at Balmoral in April 1912, and his very controversial speech at Blenheim Palace in which he committed himself to supporting the Ulster unionists in the use of 'all means in their power, including force', raised the political temperature considerably. 'Ulster Day' in September 1912, and the propaganda surrounding the signing of the Solemn League and Covenant, were extremely effective in raising British awareness of the Ulster unionists' cause. Alan O'Day, in *Irish Home Rule*, highlights the significant propaganda work of the unionists in Great Britain during the Home Rule Bill crisis: 6 million booklets were distributed, 9,000 public meetings were organised, and 1.5 million voters were canvassed to support the unionist cause. Daniel Jackson, in his book *Popular Opposition to Irish Home Rule*, highlights the support won in parts of Britain for the unionist campaign. Redmond and the nationalist politicians failed to realise the significance of the Ulster unionist campaign, and they failed to counter it.

The answer shows how the Ulster unionists opposed Home Rule. It helps to explain how they managed to fight effectively in a situation where they seemed certain to be the 'losers' in the Home Rule crisis.

Unknown to Redmond, Liberal government ministers held secret talks with Bonar Law from September 1913, and then with Carson. Public opinion in Britain was forcing Asquith's government towards a compromise based on some degree of exclusion of at least part of Ulster from Home Rule. On the other hand, British public opinion was so focused on Ulster that Bonar Law and Carson were both obliged to reconsider their opposition to Home Rule. By the end of 1913 Bonar Law, Carson and Craig were agreed that they should concentrate the fight against Home Rule on securing the exclusion of six Ulster counties.

It was not until his meeting with Asquith in February 1914 that Redmond finally realised that he was not going to secure Home Rule for all of Ireland. When Asquith pointed out to him that some degree of exclusion was unavoidable, Redmond was 'visibly perturbed' and 'shivered visibly'. He had assumed that he would be the 'winner' in the Home Rule crisis, and had no fall-back position. Mansergh, and Alvin Jackson in *Ireland*, show that the relationship between the IPP and the leading Liberal ministers was very weak. The IPP communicated with the government through the chief secretary for Ireland, Augustine Birrell, but Lloyd George and Churchill had become key players on Irish affairs in the cabinet. Both of them were convinced of the need for some form of exclusion. It is surprising that the IPP failed to interpret Churchill's meaning in his speech at Dundee in October 1913. Redmond might be forgiven for letting himself be deceived by Joe Devlin, MP for West Belfast, as to the threat posed by the UVF, yet he does appear to have been very naïve and complacent throughout the Home Rule crisis.

From February 1914 Redmond could no longer feel like a 'winner'. He was forced to make concessions about excluding four counties from Home Rule — for 3, 5 and finally 6 years. Even that was not enough for Carson, who insisted on six counties being excluded permanently. That was the unionists' demand at the Buckingham Palace conference in July 1914. Carson and Craig were strengthened by the 'Curragh mutiny', after which the British government promised that the British Army would not be deployed against the UVF, and the Larne gun-running. Many nationalists grew convinced that 'Carsonism' was winning, while Redmond's constitutionalist politics were losing.

🖉 **The turning of the tide against the nationalists is shown clearly, and Redmond's inability to influence events is highlighted.**

Redmond used the opportunity of the outbreak of the Great War to pledge nationalist support for Britain's war effort. Carson and Craig pledged the support of the UVF. Yet Redmond was rewarded in September 1914 by the passing of the Government of Ireland Act (1914). Ireland was finally to secure Home Rule. Alvin Jackson, in *Ireland*, declares that Redmond had won 'a form of triumph' by the passing of the Government of Ireland Act (1914). IPP and Labour MPs celebrated in the Commons and waved an Irish flag in the House. Redmond and the IPP appeared to be the winners. Jackson writes that the Ulster unionists were 'wounded by the enactment of Home Rule and the absence of any definite arrangement for the exclusion of Ulster'.

However, there were two key provisos to the Government of Ireland Act (1914). First, it was not to come into effect until the Great War had ended, and second, it would only come into force when 'special provision' had been made for Ulster. Carson and

Craig were angry that the 'special provision' for Ulster was not defined. Nonetheless, Craig and the Ulster unionists in the northeast were the real winners in the Third Home Rule Bill crisis. Back in 1910 Home Rule for all of Ireland seemed inevitable, but thanks to the Ulster unionists' campaign some form of exclusion for part of Ulster was conceded by the Liberal government and by the IPP. The Buckingham Palace conference made it clear that the Ulster unionists could be confident of securing Counties Antrim and Londonderry, and most of Counties Down and Armagh, and at least parts of Tyrone and Fermanagh. The government and nationalists conceded the principle of exclusion for 6 years — but effectively that would have meant that partition would be permanent. Once Carson and Craig joined the coalition government in May 1915, it was virtually certain that six counties would be excluded from Home Rule indefinitely. They were set to be the 'winners'.

Redmond was set to be a 'loser' in the sense that he had to agree to partition. However, Carson too was a 'loser' in the sense that he too had to accept partition and that meant sacrificing all of the southern unionists, his own community, and the Ulster unionists in Donegal, Cavan and Monaghan. For unionists outside the six counties, and for nationalists in the six counties, partition was the worst-case scenario. Craig and the unionists living in the future Northern Ireland were set to be the ultimate winners of the Home Rule crisis.

The passing of the Government of Ireland Act (1914) is clearly shown to have been a qualified success for Redmond and the nationalists. There is a nuanced discussion of the ambiguities of the Act with its two provisos, which gave the impression that the nationalists were the 'winners' as they had secured their long-term goal of devolution, when in fact the Ulster unionists in the northeast had succeeded in ensuring that their wishes were taken into account by the British government. The conclusion points out that the real 'losers' included not only the nationalists, despite their apparent victory in September 1914, but the Irish unionists outside the future Northern Ireland.

■ ■ ■

Question 2

'The settlement of Ireland in 1921 satisfied no one.' To what extent would you agree with this statement? Use relevant evidence you have studied, including contemporary and later interpretations, to support your answer. (35 marks)

■ ■ ■

High A-grade answer

I disagree with the proposition that the settlement of Ireland in 1921 'satisfied no one'. Nationalists in Northern Ireland and unionists in the Irish Free State were extremely dissatisfied. Southern nationalists were deeply divided about the settlement, and fought a civil war about it in 1922–23. However, unionists in Northern Ireland could be reasonably 'satisfied' with the settlement, even though they were worried about the Boundary Commission authorised by the Anglo–Irish Treaty. Also, the settlement satisfied the British government and it was supported by an overwhelming majority of British MPs in the Commons.

> 🖉 **The introduction addresses the question directly and it indicates what the argument of the essay will be. It identifies the key players, and outlines who was 'satisfied' and who was not.**

Southern nationalists, represented by Sinn Féin since the general election of 1918, were mostly dissatisfied with the Anglo–Irish Treaty of December 1921. The settlement did not match what Paul Bew, in *The Politics of Enmity*, calls 'their very high level of expectancy'. The treaty allowed all of Ireland to leave the UK, but Northern Ireland was allowed to opt out of the settlement and remain in the UK. Furthermore, the Irish Free State had to remain in the British Commonwealth and its government ministers and MPs had to swear an oath of fealty to the Crown.

The treaty sharply divided nationalists. Collins, Griffith and other pro-treaty members of Sinn Féin emphasised the tangible freedom secured through the treaty and argued that no better deal was possible at that time. Collins declared that the treaty gave Ireland 'freedom, not the ultimate freedom...but the freedom to achieve it'. De Valera's *Document No. 2* was dismissed by Collins as 'splitting hairs', and Griffith said it was only a 'quibble' about words. Belfast-born Seán MacEntee was the only TD who spoke out about partition. The dispute in Sinn Féin centred on Ireland's association with the Crown and the commonwealth. It was a matter of symbolism — but, as Richard English in *Irish Freedom* acknowledges, symbols were important to nationalists, and to the British government, who insisted on Irish consent to the Crown and empire.

The Sinn Féin cabinet split 4 to 3 in favour of the treaty. The Dáil split 64 in favour and 57 against. Yet in the country at large, public opinion was strongly in favour of the treaty. In the June 1922 general elections pro-treaty Sinn Féin won 58 seats, as opposed to 36 anti-treaty TDs, while the other 34 TDs also supported the treaty.

Michael Hopkinson, using contemporary sources in *Green Against Green*, finds little enthusiasm for the treaty among nationalists. Most were 'satisfied' with it as the best that could be achieved.

However, as Hopkinson states, a split in the IRA about the treaty led to civil war. Most of the active IRA volunteers opposed the treaty. Joe Lee in *Ireland*, and Laffan in *Partition of Ireland*, highlight the anti-democratic mentality of the anti-treaty IRA commanders like Tom Barry, Liam Mellows and Rory O'Connor, who fought against the treaty regardless of public opinion. However, English reminds us of the sincerity of the anti-treaty feeling — that the Republic had been betrayed by a treaty that consented to Ireland's membership of the British empire. In the event, the Provisional Government set up after the treaty carried the day. It deployed the resources of the Free State to win the war, but it succeeded chiefly because it enjoyed legitimacy in the eyes of the public, who were 'satisfied' with the argument that nothing more could be won by violence.

> 🖉 **The divided nationalist responses to the Anglo–Irish Treaty, and the drift to civil war, are explained. The degree to which even those nationalists who supported the treaty were not truly 'satisfied' with it is made clear.**

Nationalists in Northern Ireland were extremely dissatisfied with the settlement of Ireland. Their fears were expressed by Joe Devlin MP in the Commons. Éamon Phoenix, in *Northern Nationalism*, shows how Devlin and other nationalists in the northeast had desperately hoped that 'exclusion' from Irish Home Rule would be temporary. They saw the creation of a Northern Irish state, a 'Protestant state for a Protestant people' (as Craig later described it), as the worst possible outcome to the 'Irish Question'.

Nationalists in border areas hoped that the Boundary Commission authorised by the Anglo–Irish treaty would bring them into the Free State, but such hopes would be disappointed. Northern Ireland was born in the middle of IRA and sectarian violence. Peter Hart, in *The IRA at War*, shows how Catholics in Belfast managed to survive a 'pogrom' by loyalists, through a combination of self-help and aggressive self-defence. Yet the violent birth of Northern Ireland left deep scars. The northern state became what Patrick Buckland calls a 'factory of grievances'. A large minority of the people of Northern Ireland were left very dissatisfied.

> 🖉 **The discussion of the Northern nationalists establishes their dissatisfaction with the 'settlement' of 1921 and explains why they were so dissatisfied. It uses historiography to indicate the depth of that dissatisfaction, and to discuss the violent circumstances in which Northern Ireland was created.**

For unionists in the Irish Free State the settlement was no less unsatisfactory. They found themselves outside the UK. Hart, in *The IRA at War*, calculates that during the Anglo–Irish War and the civil war, 100 Protestants were killed by the IRA as 'spies' or 'informers'. He shows that 34% of Protestants in County Cork, the centre of IRA activity, emigrated between 1920 and 1923. IRA intimidation, and the withdrawal of the British security forces, made them feel vulnerable.

> 🖉 **The short discussion of the unionists in the Irish Free State reflects their relatively small number, the facts of their abandonment by the Ulster unionists in Northern Ireland, and their political powerlessness after 1918.**

Ulster unionists had good reason to be satisfied with the settlement of 1921. Though Craig was worried that the talks between Lloyd George and Sinn Féin might undermine the Home Rule government set up in Belfast under the Government of Ireland Act (1920), the status of Northern Ireland was copper-fastened by the Anglo–Irish Treaty. Accepting partition had meant compromising the unionists' ideal of preventing any of Ireland securing Home Rule. However, Charles Craig MP, brother of the leading Ulster unionist, James Craig, pointed out in the House of Commons debate about the 'Fourth Home Rule bill' in 1920 that the Ulster unionists were 'satisfied' to have their own government in Northern Ireland. Despite the irony of welcoming Home Rule for themselves, they saw it as a means of achieving their primary goal of having themselves excluded from the authority of a nationalist government. It came at a time of growing distance between the Ulster unionists and their Conservative allies in Great Britain, and the unionists were afraid that the Conservatives might appease the Irish nationalists to preserve the UK.

A major reason why the Ulster unionists were so satisfied with the Government of Ireland Act (1920) is that it had been decisively influenced by James Craig, as shown by a number of historians, especially Nicholas Mansergh in his book *Nationalism*, and by Graham Walker in his *History of the Ulster Unionist Party*. Craig forced the Lloyd George government, against its better judgement, to create a Northern Ireland of six counties. He felt that nine counties would have too many nationalists to control and might lead to Irish unity in the future. In May 1920 Craig persuaded the Ulster Unionist Council to support the six-county option, by 310 votes to 80. Most Ulster unionists were 'satisfied'. Alvin Jackson in *Ireland* observes that to secure their own self-preservation the Ulster unionists in Northern Ireland were willing to abandon the Southern unionists, and even Ulster unionists in Donegal, Cavan and Monaghan. Walker, and Bardon in his *History of Ulster*, show that Ulster unionists in those three counties were deeply dissatisfied at being abandoned, as reflected in their pamphlet, *The Partition of Ulster*. Yet from 1913 Craig and Carson decided that they would be 'satisfied' with six counties.

Craig was worried about the potential of the Boundary Commission to undermine Northern Ireland, but he was assured by Lloyd George that the commission would make only minor changes to the border. Events in 1925 proved that Lloyd George was correct. In fact, the Anglo–Irish Treaty forced Sinn Féin to accept the reality of partition and there was hardly any mention of partition during the treaty debates in the Dáil. In effect, the settlement of 1921 could hardly have been better from the point of view of Craig and other unionists in Northern Ireland.

The British government had most reason to be satisfied with the settlement of 1921. Alvin Jackson argues that there was 'a growing British desire for disengagement' from Ireland. By June 1921 the British government decided to make major concessions to Sinn Féin, as long as its own priorities on the Crown, empire, security and Ulster were satisfied. The main outlines of the settlement embodied in the Anglo–Irish Treaty were agreed by Lloyd George's cabinet before the truce was called in July 1921. Foster points out that Lloyd George's hands were 'tied' before the negotiations with Sinn Féin. Nonetheless, the British government was satisfied with the Anglo–Irish Treaty, and it was supported by an overwhelming majority of British MPs in the Commons.

In conclusion, it is not true to say that the settlement of 1921 'satisfied no one'. The British government and public were satisfied with what they considered as the resolution of the Irish question. Ulster unionists in Northern Ireland were more than 'satisfied' to have a state of their own. Everyone else was dissatisfied to varying degrees. The settlement left nationalists in the North and unionists in the South extremely dissatisfied, and it split nationalists in the South so badly that it led to civil war.

The conclusion addresses the question posed directly again and offers a clear summation of its argument.

■ ■ ■